GREAT WONDERS
OF THE WORLD

Written by RUSSELL ASH
Illustrated by RICHARD BONSON

A DORLING KINDERSLEY BOOK

DORLING KINDERSLEY

LONDON, NEW YORK, SYDNEY, DELHI, PARIS,
MUNICH and JOHANNESBURG

Project Editor Amanda Rayner
Project Art Editor Lester Cheeseman
Art Editor Rebecca Johns
Editorial Advisor Susan Malyan
Managing Editor Mary Ling
Managing Art Editor Rachael Foster
DTP Designer Almudena Díaz
Picture Research Andrea Sadler
Jacket Design Karen Shooter
Production Ruth Cobb, Orla Creegan

Ancient History Consultant George Hart, British Museum
Research Assistant Aylla Macphail

First published in Great Britain in 2000
by Dorling Kindersley Limited
9 Henrietta Street, London WC2E 8PS

2 4 6 8 10 9 7 5 3 1

A CIP catalogue record for this book
is available from the British Library

ISBN 0 7513 2886 3

Color reproduction by Colourscan, Singapore
Printed and bound in Spain by Artes Gráficas Toledo, S.A.U.
D.L. TO: 667 - 2000

See our complete
catalogue at
www.dk.com

CONTENTS

A HISTORY OF WONDERS

THE SEVEN WONDERS OF THE WORLD make up one of the best-known lists ever compiled, yet few people can name them all. The number seven has long held a special meaning, but why was this particular group of seven chosen? The first mention of the Seven Wonders was in the 5th century BC, when the Greek historian Herodotus drew up a list of admired buildings that included the Pyramids and the Hanging Gardens of Babylon. He was followed by a mathematician named Philo of Byzantium around 225 BC and the Greek writer, Antipater of Sidon, around 130 BC. They drew up their lists before the Pharos of Alexandria was built, so they included the Walls of Babylon instead.

By the Middle Ages, the full list had been generally agreed, but of those seven superb structures, only the Great Pyramid is still standing today. The others were destroyed, and descriptions and ruins are all that remain. This book looks at each of the Seven Wonders and compares them with other great structures. It also includes many other "wonders", from important inventions and triumphs of engineering to weird and natural wonders.

MAP OF THE SEVEN WONDERS
Greek writers listed the Seven Wonders from among the structures on their own doorstep, and all of them were sited within Alexander the Great's empire. They included the Great Pyramid at Giza, the Statue of Zeus at Clympia, the Mausoleum at Halicarnassus (a tomb), the Hanging Gardens of Babylon, the Colossus of Rhodes (a giant statue), the Pharos at Alexandria (a lighthouse), and the Temple of Artemis at Ephesus.

WHY BUILD A WONDER?
In ancient times, important people built magnificent structures as visible proof of their power and influence. No one could fail to be impressed by the skills involved in their construction, and their existence was a source of great pride for local people. Religious devotion also played a significant part in the development of many of the Wonders, and all seven structures became popular tourist attractions.

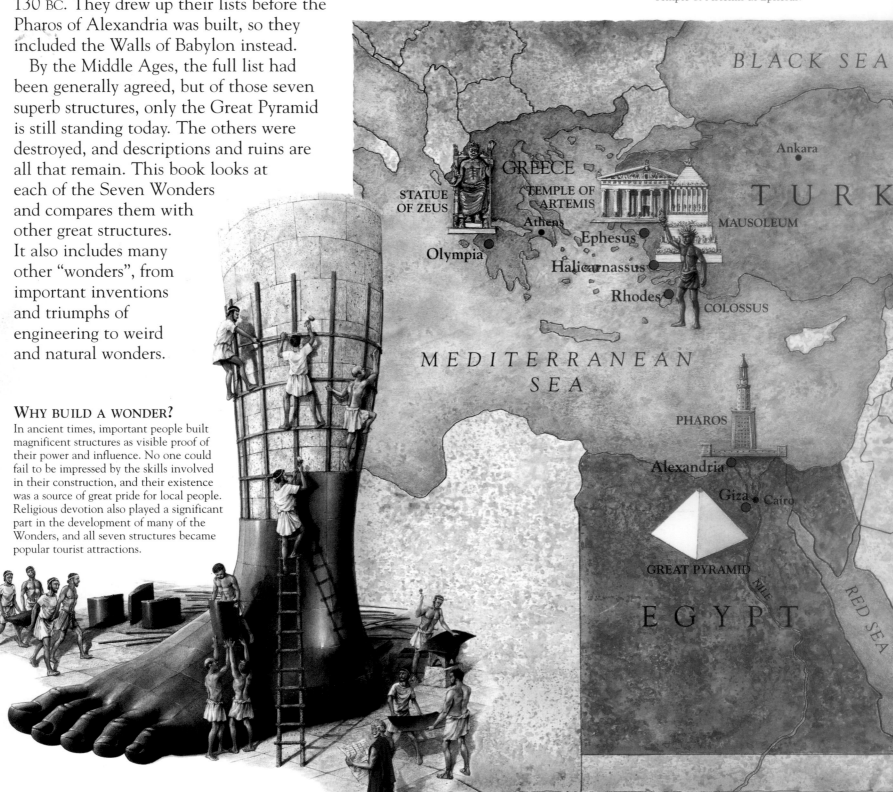

4

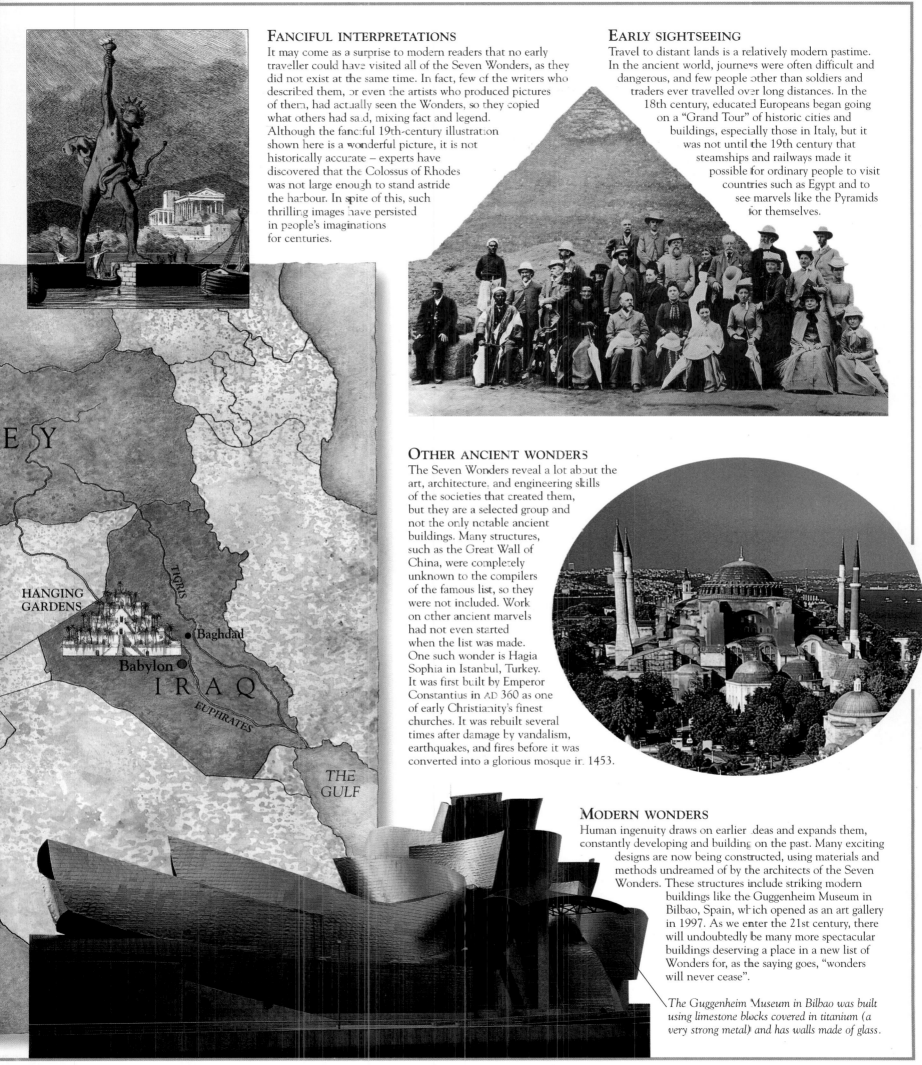

FANCIFUL INTERPRETATIONS

It may come as a surprise to modern readers that no early traveller could have visited all of the Seven Wonders, as they did not exist at the same time. In fact, few of the writers who described them, or even the artists who produced pictures of them, had actually seen the Wonders, so they copied what others had said, mixing fact and legend. Although the fanciful 19th-century illustration shown here is a wonderful picture, it is not historically accurate – experts have discovered that the Colossus of Rhodes was not large enough to stand astride the harbour. In spite of this, such thrilling images have persisted in people's imaginations for centuries.

EARLY SIGHTSEEING

Travel to distant lands is a relatively modern pastime. In the ancient world, journeys were often difficult and dangerous, and few people other than soldiers and traders ever travelled over long distances. In the 18th century, educated Europeans began going on a "Grand Tour" of historic cities and buildings, especially those in Italy, but it was not until the 19th century that steamships and railways made it possible for ordinary people to visit countries such as Egypt and to see marvels like the Pyramids for themselves.

OTHER ANCIENT WONDERS

The Seven Wonders reveal a lot about the art, architecture, and engineering skills of the societies that created them, but they are a selected group and not the only notable ancient buildings. Many structures, such as the Great Wall of China, were completely unknown to the compilers of the famous list, so they were not included. Work on other ancient marvels had not even started when the list was made. One such wonder is Hagia Sophia in Istanbul, Turkey. It was first built by Emperor Constantius in AD 360 as one of early Christianity's finest churches. It was rebuilt several times after damage by vandalism, earthquakes, and fires before it was converted into a glorious mosque in 1453.

HANGING GARDENS

TIGRIS

• Baghdad

Babylon ○

I R A Q

EUPHRATES

THE GULF

E Y

MODERN WONDERS

Human ingenuity draws on earlier ideas and expands them, constantly developing and building on the past. Many exciting designs are now being constructed, using materials and methods undreamed of by the architects of the Seven Wonders. These structures include striking modern buildings like the Guggenheim Museum in Bilbao, Spain, which opened as an art gallery in 1997. As we enter the 21st century, there will undoubtedly be many more spectacular buildings deserving a place in a new list of Wonders for, as the saying goes, "wonders will never cease".

The Guggenheim Museum in Bilbao was built using limestone blocks covered in titanium (a very strong metal) and has walls made of glass.

THE GREAT PYRAMID AT GIZA

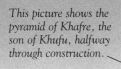

THE GREAT PYRAMID AT GIZA IN EGYPT is the only one of the Seven Wonders of the Ancient World that is still standing today. For almost 4,000 years it was the world's tallest building – on completion it was a staggering 147 m (481 ft) in height. It is also the largest and most precisely constructed stone structure ever built. Standing on the western bank of the River Nile, it was built for King Khufu, the second ruler of the Fourth Dynasty, who is sometimes known by the Greek name "Cheops". Khufu ruled from around 2551 to 2528 BC and supervised the building of his pyramid to serve as his tomb. Although it was based on his father's pyramid at Dahshur, it is much bigger, and heralded the great period of pyramid building. There were other pyramids before the Great Pyramid, and more were built later, but no structure has so fascinated the world for more than four millennia.

This picture shows the pyramid of Khafre, the son of Khufu, halfway through construction.

Made of mud bricks, the ramp grew steadily in height as layers were added and the pyramid progressed. The ramp was later removed.

Stone blocks were dragged on sledges with wooden rollers underneath. As they were pulled forwards, the roller from the back was moved to the front, and so on.

KHUFU THE KING

Although his name is recorded above the King's Chamber, no other trace of Khufu has been found inside the Great Pyramid, as his mummy was stolen by tomb robbers. The only statue known to be of him is this small ivory figurine, found buried in rubble hundreds of kilometres to the south.

The pyramid belonging to Menkaure, one of the pharaohs buried at Giza, was the smallest of the three main pyramids. It was built around 2490 BC and was 65 m (213 ft) high.

Alongside the pyramids of Khufu and Menkaure are groups of smaller pyramids. They are known as the queens' pyramids because they were probably built for the King's wives.

The causeway was used during the building of the pyramid and later roofed over to become a sacred route between the valley temple and the pyramid.

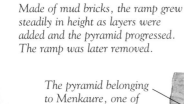

Khufu's son Khafre built his pyramid around 2520 BC. It is 143.5 m (471 ft) high.

Khufu's pyramid is known as the Great Pyramid. It is the largest of all Egyptian pyramids and the best-known of all the Seven Wonders of the Ancient World.

The Sphinx is a gigantic statue of a lion with a human head that is 20 m (66 ft) high. It was carved from solid rock around 2500 BC, during the reign of Khafre.

PYRAMID PLAN

This bird's-eye view of the pyramids of Giza shows the site looking towards the west. The area was chosen because its level rocky surface made an ideal foundation for the massive structures, and it could be quarried for building materials. A complex "city" of pyramids, temples, and houses grew up over several generations.

The valley temple was used to house the mummified body of the dead King before it was placed in the pyramid.

AMAZING FACTS

• The Great Pyramid is thought to weigh more than 5 million tonnes and is composed of more than 2 million blocks.
• It covers an area of 5.15 hectares (12.7 acres), the same as 200 tennis courts.
• St Peter's Basilica in Rome, Italy, would fit twice into the ground area occupied by the Great Pyramid.
• Napoleon calculated that the three main pyramids contained enough stone to build a wall 3 m (10 ft) high and 30 cm (1 ft) thick around the whole of France.

There is some evidence that gold leaf originally covered the tip of the pyramid. The effect would have been dazzling.

The outside of the pyramid was covered with gleaming white Tura limestone from a quarry in the Muqattam Hills, east of modern Cairo. Very little of this stone is left today.

THE PYRAMIDS TODAY

The pyramids attract large numbers of tourists. At night, dramatic sound and light shows are staged, with high-tech lasers illuminating the 4,500-year-old monuments. Restoration work and excavations go on all the time, and recent discoveries include the remains of a small "satellite" pyramid behind Khufu's queens' pyramids.

Only one of the queens' pyramids, built for Khufu's wives and sisters, is believed to have been used.

Mastabas are flat-topped tombs built for officials, courtiers, and minor members of the royal family. The name comes from the Arabic word for "bench".

Khufu's son Khafre oversaw work on his own pyramid.

An architect supervised the building of Khafre's pyramid. His identity is not certain, but he may have been the nephew of the chief-of-works on the Great Pyramid.

Farm workers helped during the months when their fields were flooded. Experts now think that 20,000 workers would have been needed to build the pyramid.

Some of the stone blocks were transported along the River Nile and up a canal. There they were unloaded and levered onto sledges.

The roughly hewn blocks of stone were "dressed", or prepared, on the site by stonemasons before being taken to the pyramid.

7

BUILDING THE PYRAMID

FOR THOUSANDS OF YEARS, people have marvelled at the Great Pyramid. How were such vast quantities of stone quarried and transported? How did workers build such an accurate structure using only primitive tools? Visitors to Giza have also been impressed by the precision of the Great Pyramid's construction. Its four sides are aligned almost exactly with true north, south, east, and west, and the difference between the longest and shortest side is only 20 cm (8 in). As the art of pyramid building was developed in ancient Egypt, so new methods were invented that were appropriate to the site, materials, and style of pyramid. Archaeologists have gradually revealed some of the builders' secrets, but many questions still remain unanswered.

THE SPIRAL RAMP OPTION

There are many different ideas of how the pyramid was built. A straight ramp leading to one face, increasing in height as the pyramid grew, is one, while another popular notion is that of a spiral ramp rising around the structure.

According to one theory, the hard rock was separated from the softer layers by hammering in wooden wedges. These were then soaked in water and expanded, splitting the layers apart.

Originally, the causeway was the road on which the stone blocks were transported. Later, its sides were built up and decorated with carvings. It was then roofed over to create a corridor along which the royal burial procession travelled from the valley temple.

LEVELLING THE SITE

The Giza plateau is a large area of limestone at the Earth's surface that provided a ready supply of building materials and formed a perfect base for building. However, before work could begin on the pyramids, the site had to be levelled to make it perfectly flat.

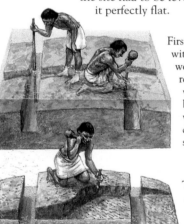

First the site was flooded with water. Trenches were then cut into the rock and measured with a stick. The base of every trench was exactly the same depth below the surface of the water.

Then the site was drained, but some water was left in the trenches. Next the surrounding rock was cut down to the same level as the water's surface.

QUARRYING THE STONE BLOCKS

The quarry that supplied most of the stone for building the Great Pyramid lay 300 m (985 ft) to the south. From it, workers removed almost 3 million cubic m (95 million cubic ft) of rock using only hand tools and levers. Tura limestone for the pyramid's surface came from quarries east of the River Nile, while granite for the King's Chamber was quarried near Aswan and brought down the river.

To move the stone blocks, workers used ropes and levers. Experts think that at least 1,200 men would have been needed to quarry enough blocks to build the Great Pyramid.

The King's body was taken to the mortuary temple for religious ceremonies before being carried into the burial chamber in the pyramid.

HISTORY OF THE PYRAMID

Mastaba
Forerunners of the great Egyptian pyramids, these flat-topped tombs were for officials, courtiers, and minor royals. At first they were made of mud bricks, but later stone was used.

Step Pyramid at Saqqara
The first stone pyramid was built around 2630 BC in three stages – a large mastaba, followed by a four-stepped and a six-stepped pyramid. It is 60 m (197 ft) high, with a base 140 x 118 m (459 x 387 ft).

Bent Pyramid at Dahshur
This was the first attempt, around 2560 BC, to build a pyramid with smooth sides, rather than steps. Architects discovered too late that the angle was wrong, so they made it less steep in the upper part.

North Pyramid at Dahshur
After the Bent Pyramid was abandoned, the North or Red Pyramid was built nearby. It was the first pyramid to be built successfully with straight sides. Khufu's father, Sneferu, may have been buried there.

Pyramids at Giza
The Great Pyramid (built around 2550 BC), Menkaure's Pyramid, and their companion queens' pyramids, together with Khafre's pyramid, make the Giza plateau the focal point of Egyptian pyramid building.

INSIDE THE GREAT PYRAMID

The Great Pyramid contains more passageways and chambers than any other pyramid. These have all been investigated – even the air shafts were studied recently using a robotic camera – but many mysteries remain.

The King's Chamber lies almost in the centre of the pyramid.

The air shafts from the King's Chamber line up with the northern pole stars and the constellation of Orion, and were intended for the King's soul to ascend to the stars.

Above the King's Chamber are five "relieving chambers" to spread the colossal weight of the stone above it and prevent the whole structure from collapsing.

One of the granite blocks bears the name of Khufu, while graffiti on the slabs records the names of the workers who built the chamber.

There is no evidence that the Queen's Chamber was ever used for a queen. It probably contained a statue of the King.

The Grand Gallery is 46.7 m (153 ft 3 in) long and 2.1 m (6 ft 11 in) wide.

Three granite slabs blocked the route to the King's Chamber. They were put there to deter robbers.

The entrance is on the northern face. According to one ancient writer, a secret trapdoor opened in the limestone casing.

The workers and priests left the tomb by climbing down the shaft leading to the chamber and up the descending passage. They sealed the end with granite slabs.

Five boat pits have been discovered at the site. When one of these was unearthed in 1954, it revealed a wooden boat.

This underground chamber may have been intended as a burial chamber, but it was never completed.

KING'S CHAMBER

Hidden within the Great Pyramid is the King's Chamber. Exactly twice as long as it is wide – 10.6 m x 5.3 m (34 ft 4 in x 17 ft 2 in), it is 5.9 m (19 ft 1 in) high, and has a flat roof. The lower roof is made of nine huge granite blocks, each weighing 40 tonnes.

Khufu's sarcophagus cannot be removed since it is slightly larger than the entrance to the chamber! This shows that the pyramid was constructed around the sarcophagus. The King's body and treasure were later stolen by tomb robbers.

FUNERAL BOAT

This model of a funeral boat is similar to the boat found in the boat pit. The boat, which was made of more than 1 200 pieces of wood, had been sealed in its chamber and was perfectly preserved. Now reassembled, it measures 43.3 m (142 ft) in length. It may have been used to convey Khufu's body along the Nile to its final resting place

Pyramids at Meroe
From the 6th century BC to the 2nd century AD, Meroe was the capital of an African state in what is now Sudan. From around 300 BC to AD 350 its kings were buried beneath small, steep-sided pyramids.

Pyramid of the Sun, Teotihuacán
This massive pyramid, situated 40 km (25 miles) north east of Mexico City, contains an even greater volume of stone than the Great Pyramid at Giza. It was built around AD 150 and is 66 m (216 ft) high.

Castillo at Chichén Itzá
The Castillo is a pyramid built between AD 900 and AD 1200 in the Mayan city of Chichén Itzá, Mexico. Priests conducted religious ceremonies in the temple at the top level, reached by staircases on all four sides.

The Great Temple, Tenochtitlán
This Aztec temple-pyramid in what is now Mexico City was dedicated to the gods Tlaloc and Huitzilopochtli. Thousands of victims were sacrificed to the gods in the two temples at the top of the pyramid.

Glass pyramid Louvre, Paris
Reviving the tradition of pyramid building, Chinese-born American architect I. M. Pei's 22-m (71-ft) glass pyramid, built in 1989, is the principal entrance to the Louvre Museum, Paris France.

SPECTACULAR PYRAMIDS

THE PYRAMID SHAPE has inspired builders since ancient times, surprisingly in cultures that had no direct contact with each other, such as those of north Africa and Central America. During a span of almost 5,000 years pyramids arose for purposes that ranged from tombs to religious rituals. They were often the tallest structures of the civilizations that created them, and people who saw them would have marvelled at their scale. Their simple yet impressive appearance has continued to fascinate architects, and the 20th century saw a revival of pyramid-style buildings, used for everything from offices to hotels.

ZIGGURAT AT UR
The people of ancient Sumer (present-day Iraq) built many pyramid-like structures, called ziggurats. These were erected in a series of step-like layers, and the most complete example is this one at Ur (now in southern Iraq). This temple was built entirely of mud bricks around 2100 BC and has recently been partly reconstructed. The ziggurats contained fabulous treasures, some of which have been unearthed by archaeologists.

The doorway to the temple chamber was made to look like a giant mask of Chac, the Maya god of rain.

STEP PYRAMID AT SAQQARA
This was the first stone pyramid ever built and is situated at Saqqara, to the south of Giza, in Egypt. The Step Pyramid was built as a tomb for the ruler Djoser, who reigned from 2630 to 2611 BC, and was designed by the great architect, Imhotep. Archaeologists have found an impressive statue of Djoser outside the pyramid as well as beautiful carvings in underground galleries.

The stairway on the structure's west side has now been restored.

NUBIAN PYRAMIDS AT MEROE
The last pyramids to be built as royal tombs, the Nubian pyramids at Meroe (now part of Sudan) were steep-sided sandstone structures. These pyramids, which were built for the Nubian pharaohs, were up to 30 m (98 ft) tall and many were decorated with carvings. Inside, the mummified bodies of kings and queens were placed in elaborate coffins, along with the bodies of servants sacrificed to accompany them in the afterlife.

PYRAMID OF THE MAGICIAN
Uxmal on the Yucatán peninsula of Mexico was a city built by the Maya people between AD 700 and 1000. It was abandoned in the 15th century. According to legend, the 39-m (128-ft) Pyramid of the Magician was built in a single night by the sorcerer-god Itzamna. However, evidence found by archaeologists shows that it was actually built in five stages. The centre of Uxmal was important in religion and magic and is aligned with the planets that were known at the time; for example, the stairway on the west side of the Pyramid faces the setting Sun on the longest day of the year.

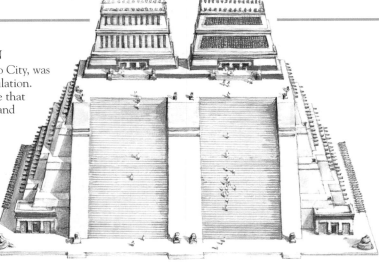

GREAT TEMPLE OF TENOCHTITLÁN

The Aztec capital of Tenochtitlán, now Mexico City, was once a centre of government, with a large population. In the middle of the city was a walled enclosure that contained many temples. This was the biggest and most important one. Although impressive, at a height of 30 m (98 ft) this structure was only a fifth as tall as the Great Pyramid at Giza. At the top were two temples. The first was dedicated to Huitzilopochtli, the god of war and the Sun, and human sacrifice to him was believed to make the Sun rise each day. The second temple was dedicated to Tlaloc, the god of rain. His worship was important to ensure good harvests.

LUXOR HOTEL

Opened in 1993 at a cost of £229 million, the Luxor Hotel in Las Vegas, USA, is 107 m (350 ft) tall and has 4,400 rooms. As well as a 1,100-seat arena and an enormous casino, it contains an Olympic-sized swimming pool and an imitation River Nile complete with pleasure boats and talking model camels. Even the lifts are remarkable, travelling along a steep diagonal at 39 degrees to match the slope of the pyramid. The light at the top of the building is so bright that some people claim that it is visible from outer space. One of the hotel's strangest features is the sphinx guarding the entrance that shoots laser beams from its eyes.

An aircraft warning light at the tip of the spire is one of the building's many safety features.

Aluminium panels cover the spire, and the lower portion contains mechanical equipment

From the top floor there are breathtaking views of San Francisco's other landmarks, including the Golden Gate Bridge.

Two wings rise from the 29th floor, housing lifts, a stairwell, and a smoke tower.

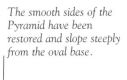

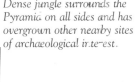

The smooth sides of the Pyramid have been restored and slope steeply from the oval base.

Dense jungle surrounds the Pyramid on all sides and has overgrown other nearby sites of archaeological interest.

The architects, William L. Pereira & Associates, erected the Pyramid using concrete, glass, and steel. Its flexible frame allows the building to absorb vibrations caused by earthquakes in the surrounding area.

TRANSAMERICA PYRAMID

The international headquarters of the Transamerica Corporation is the tallest building in San Francisco, USA. Completed in 1972, it has 48 storeys and a total height of 260 m (853 ft), of which 65 m (212 ft) consists of a spire covered in aluminium panels, with an aircraft warning light on the tip. It was designed to withstand earthquakes, which can topple tall buildings in a matter of seconds, and its pyramid shape allows plenty of light to reach street level. Although it looks enormous, its base area is smaller than that of the Great Pyramid at Giza.

THE STATUE OF ZEUS AT OLYMPIA

IN 433 BC, A SCULPTOR CALLED PHIDIAS finished work on an incredible statue of Zeus, the king of the Greek gods. Housed in a specially built temple at Olympia in southern Greece, the statue was a gigantic 13 m (43 ft) tall – higher than a modern four-storey house. The statue cost a fortune as it was made of many precious materials, including a tonne of ivory and even more gold.

The statue's size and its creator's astonishing attention to detail amazed all visitors; it was said to be more like a piece of jewellery than a sculpture. Phidias showed Zeus seated on his throne, and the form was so lifelike that many people believed they had seen the actual god. The statue remained in the Temple for centuries but was neglected during Roman times. Some parts of the statue were said to have been rescued in AD 394 and taken to Constantinople (now Istanbul) in Turkey, where they were destroyed in a fire.

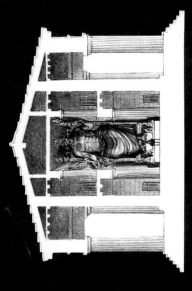

CROSS-SECTION

The Temple of Zeus was built around 466–456 BC. There were 13 columns along each side and six at the ends. The architect used local limestone, which was covered with plaster, and marble roof tiles.

GREECE
• Athens
OLYMPIA
MEDITERRANEAN SEA

A splendid eagle made of gold perched on top of Zeus's sceptre. This was a sign of the god's power.

Important visitors could view the statue's head close up by climbing a spiral staircase to a gallery, which may have been located here.

Zeus's eyes, inlaid with coloured glass, were said to be particularly realistic.

The sceptre in Zeus's left hand was inlaid with precious metals. It was probably made of gold-covered wood.

The Three Graces were sister goddesses said to give beauty and charm to fortunate humans. The daughters of Zeus and the goddess Eurynome, they were called Aglaea, Thalia and Euphrosyne.

Zeus's golden olive wreath showed his connection with the Olympian athletes; winners at the Games were also crowned with olive wreaths.

Nike, the winged goddess of victory, appears as Zeus's constant companion in Greek mythology. Here she is a figure in gold and ivory, standing on his right hand.

The gigantic throne was made of cedarwood and adorned with gold, precious stones, ebony, and ivory.

Phidias began work by building a wooden frame for the statue. This was covered with panels of ivory for the flesh and panels of gold for the clothes. It was then decorated with enamel, glass, and jewels. Figures made from these materials were known as chryselephantine statues.

Only the priests of the Temple were allowed to approach the holy statue. Ordinary visitors had to view it from a distance, glimpsing it when a priest pulled aside a curtain.

AMAZING FACTS

- The statue took Phidias eight years to complete.
- The writer Strabo calculated that if Zeus had been able to stand up, his head would have gone through the Temple roof!
- The statue's ivory came from elephants' tusks and hippopotamuses' teeth. It was oiled to protect it from dampness or from cracking in the summer heat.
- At today's prices the gold used in the statue would cost more than £6 million.
- The Roman Emperor Caligula tried to steal the statue, but his workmen fled in terror when, according to legend, it laughed at them and their scaffolding collapsed.

The Sphinx was a legendary monster whose upper part was that of a woman and lower part a lion. It also had the tail of a snake and the wings of a bird.

Zeus's robe was made of sheets of gold that had been beaten into shape. In Phidias's workshop, archaeologists discovered a collection of clay moulds that may have been used to shape sections of Zeus's costume.

Zeus is shown wearing golden sandals. According to the writer Pausanias, inscribed under the sandals were the words "Athenian Phidias, the son of Charmides, made me".

A carved lion supported each side of Zeus's footstool.

Floral designs, including lilies, decorated the throne on which the statue of Zeus sat.

Athletes left gifts at the shrine to ensure victory in the Games. According to legend, the bronze urn in which athletes placed sacrifices was positioned on the spot that Zeus struck with a bolt of lightning to show Phidias that he approved of the statue.

OLYMPIA

FOR HUNDREDS OF YEARS worshippers made offerings to Zeus at Olympia. By the 5th century BC the site was one of the holiest places in Greece, and the Olympic Games took place there once every four years as part of a religious celebration. The Games included many exciting events such as running, jumping, throwing, wrestling, boxing, and chariot racing, and they were so important that even regional wars were halted as cities competed against each other for prestige. Only free-born Greeks were allowed to take part, and competitors trained for each event from childhood. Victorious athletes were allowed to dedicate a statue to the gods, and by the final Olympic celebration 3,000 such statues stood in a sacred enclosure called the *altis*, which also contained the temples of Zeus and his wife Hera. The last Games were held in AD 393, and it was more than 1,500 years before the modern Olympics began.

PRESENT-DAY SITE

Earthquakes, deliberate destruction, and the passing of time have turned the once great Olympia into a field of ruins, which was buried in river silt to a depth of 5 m (16 ft). However, modern excavations, together with the detailed descriptions of ancient writers, have helped experts to discover a great deal about the site and the Games that took place there.

The gymnasium had a courtyard with two practice running tracks and an area large enough for javelin and discus throwing.

The palaestra was a training ground for wrestling and boxing built at the end of the 3rd century BC.

The only open-air swimming pool in ancient Greece was probably built in the 5th century BC.

Phidias's workshop was the same height as the Temple of Zeus, so the sculptor could test the statue before assembling it in its home.

PLAN OF OLYMPIA

Archaeologists have uncovered the locations and layouts of many of the buildings at Olympia. Each of the cities competing at the Games erected its own splendid treasury, or shrine, and their remains lie beneath the Hill of Kronos on the north side of the *altis*. Spectators would have crowded around the stadium to share in the excitement of each race, and archaeologists have found the original starting line. Chariot racing was one of the last events to be introduced to the Games, so the *hippodrome* was a more recent addition to the site.

The Temple of Hera was built in the 8th century BC and was the oldest temple at Olympia.

There were 12 treasuries managed by Greek cities. They contained holy objects left there for safekeeping.

Oaks and olive trees covered the Hill of Kronos, which was named after the father of Zeus.

The leonidaeum acted as a guesthouse for important visitors to Olympia. It was constructed in 330–320 BC. The building measured 80 x 74 m (262 x 243 ft) and was erected around a courtyard with gardens and fountains.

The Temple of Zeus was the most important shrine at Olympia and the home of Phidias's great statue.

SPORT

Discus throwing, along with running, jumping, javelin throwing, and wrestling, formed the *pentathlon* – five events that decided the greatest all-round athlete. This became part of the Olympics in 708 BC. From about this time onwards, competitors took part completely naked.

The stadium was the focus for the main athletic events and attracted as many as 40,000 spectators. It was said to be the longest track in ancient Greece.

The hippodrome was where horse events took place (hippos means horse). It was an oval track with sharp turns at each end where up to 10 four-horse chariots competed in dangerous races.

At the starting gates a metal dolphin fell and the form of an eagle rose to signal the beginning of a race.

FAMILY OF GODS

The ancient Greeks believed that there were many gods, each of whom had influence over a particular aspect of life. The 12 most important gods, known as the Olympians, were said to live on Mount Olympus (not to be confused with the site of Olympia, over which they also ruled). Many beautiful temples were built to honour the most powerful among this family of gods and goddesses.

Ares
The god of war and the son of Zeus and Hera, noted for his bloodthirsty ways. His symbols were the helmet and vulture.

Aphrodite
The goddess of love and beauty and the daughter of Zeus and Dione. Legend says that she was born from the sea.

Artemis
The goddess of hunting and the Moon and the daughter of Zeus and Leto. Her symbols were the spear and stag.

Zeus and Hera
Zeus was the king of the gods. The son of Kronos and Rhea, he held a thunderbolt that symbolized his power over the heavens. Hera was Zeus's wife and sister and the queen of heaven. She was the goddess of brides and was associated with peacocks. Zeus also had other partners and produced many gods and goddesses.

Apollo
The god of light and music and the son of Zeus and Leto. He rode a chariot drawn by swans and carried a lyre.

Hermes
The messenger of the gods and the son of Zeus and Maia. He carried a staff and had winged heels and a broad-brimmed hat.

Demeter
The goddess of the harvest and the daughter of Kronos and Rhea. She was traditionally shown holding ears of corn.

Hestia
The goddess of the hearth, the daughter of Kronos and Rhea, and the sister of Zeus. Her symbol was the fireplace.

Poseidon
The god of the sea and earthquakes and the brother of Zeus. He was associated with horses and carried a three-pronged spear, or trident.

Athena
The goddess of wisdom and the daughter of Zeus and Metis. She was a brave warrior who was shown with a helmet, shield, and spear.

Hephaestus
The god of fire and metalworking and the son of Zeus and Hera. He was a blacksmith whose symbol was the anvil.

SACRED STATUES

THE ANCIENT GREEKS were not the only people to create statues of their gods. Over the centuries, people of many other cultures have carved sculptures to express their spiritual beliefs. Although certain faiths, such as Islam, do not allow their followers to make sacred images, many important religious sculptures exist throughout the world. Sometimes these statues have a human form, or they may be part-human, part-animal, such as the Sphinx, or completely animal, like the Nandi bull. In some cases worshippers believe that a god inhabits the statue, and the figures themselves are worshipped. Other statues are considered to be earthly representations of gods. Sacred statues are often built on a gigantic scale in order to impress believers with their strength. But many that are no more than life-sized, such as a beautiful sculpture of Mary and Jesus, have a powerful effect on people.

The Sphinx is made of different layers of rock. Its body, made of soft rock, has eroded more quickly than its head.

CHACMOOL STATUE

This impressive stone statue reclines at the top of the Temple of the Warriors at Chichén Itzá on the Yucatán peninsula in Mexico. It dates from around AD 900–1050 and may once have been worshipped as a rain god by the Toltec people. The figure holds a bowl on its stomach, which was probably intended for the hearts of victims sacrificed during religious ceremonies. The name *chacmool* was invented by August Le Plongeon, a French archaeologist who investigated Chichén Itzá in the 1860s. He claimed that the word meant "tiger king". All statues of this type are now known as *chacmools*.

The Temple of the Warriors is surrounded by hundreds of columns carved with reliefs.

Some experts now believe that chacmool statues represented fallen warriors who acted as messengers to the gods.

CHRIST THE REDEEMER

Standing high on Corcovado mountain, which towers over Rio de Janeiro in Brazil, is a dramatic representation of Christ. The 30-m (98-ft) soapstone and concrete statue, known as Christ the Redeemer, seems to be blessing the city with open arms. It was commissioned in 1921 to celebrate 100 years of Brazilian independence and was the creation of an engineer named Hector da Silva. The statue's pedestal contains a chapel big enough for 150 people and is reached by a mountain railway and by climbing 220 steps.

MICHELANGELO'S *PIETÀ*

For five centuries pilgrims have flocked to see this statue of the Virgin Mary holding the dead body of Christ at St Peter's Basilica in Rome, Italy. *Pietà*, the name of this extraordinary statue, means "pity", and from the 15th century onwards many European artists were inspired to create images of this emotional subject. This exceptional work of art was carved out of a large block of white Tuscan marble. It was created by the Italian artist Michelangelo, who completed it in 1499, when he was only 25 years old.

THE SPHINX

In ancient Egypt, a sphinx was a mythical creature with a lion's body and a human head. The most famous surviving statue of a sphinx is located to the south of the Great Pyramid at Giza. This huge statue was carved from an outcrop of rock around 2500 BC and appears to be guarding the pyramids. The head was probably modelled on that of the god-king, Khafre, and the statue was later worshipped as the Sun god, Haremakhet. It was once covered in plaster and brightly painted, but today it is badly worn. The nose and beard have fallen off, but part of the cobra symbol on its forehead survives.

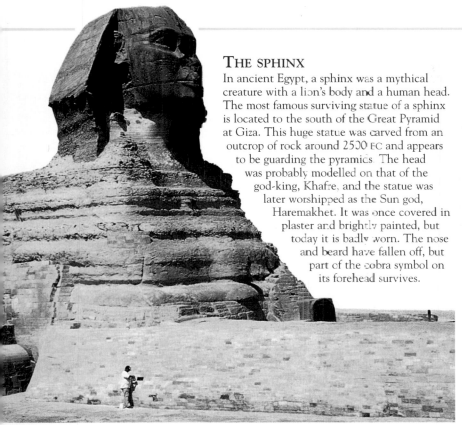

ABU SIMBEL

Around 1260 BC the Egyptian Pharaoh Ramses II had a temple carved out of the side of a mountain at Abu Simbel. Its entrance was guarded by four statues of Ramses II, each standing 20 m (66 ft) high. The ancient Egyptians believed that their king was a divine figure, and he was one of four gods worshipped in the temple. In the 1960s, engineers drew up plans to build the Aswan High Dam, which was needed to manage the region's water, and Abu Simbel was due to be covered by an artificial lake. Workers managed to preserve the statues by cutting them out in sections and moving them to higher ground, where they were reassembled.

LESHAN GIANT BUDDHA

The world's largest statue of Buddha is carved out of a cliff on Mount Lingyun, a peak near the city of Leshan in south-west China. Work on the 71-m (234-ft) Giant Buddha began in AD 713 and was completed 90 years later. The carving is so enormous that the Buddha's nose is three times taller than a person. The statue originally stood inside a 13-storey building, which has since been destroyed. The Buddha was believed to protect boatmen on the three rivers that it faces (the Min Jiang, Dadu He, and Qingyi Jiang). Sadly, the holy site has been overgrown by plants, although a restoration project has recently begun. The statue is now part of a protected cultural site.

Worshippers decorate the Nandi bull with garlands and leave offerings at the shrine.

NANDI BULL

In the Chamundi Hills near Mysore in southern India stands a huge statue of a bull, called a Nandi bull. Its name means "the happy one". This sculpture is 4.8 m (15 ft 9 in) high and is one of only seven similar statues in India. Carved from a block of granite, the Nandi bull was originally grey in colour, but many pilgrims have annointed it with oil, gradually turning it black. In Hindu mythology from the 1st century AD onwards, Nandi was closely associated with Shiva, one of the religion's most powerful gods.

THE MAUSOLEUM AT HALICARNASSUS

WITH ITS COMBINATION OF SUPERB architecture and truly magnificent sculpture, the Mausoleum of Halicarnassus must once have been an extraordinary sight. It was designed in the 4th century BC as a tomb fit for the most important man in south-western Turkey, a regional governor, called Mausolus. Work on the Mausoleum probably began while Mausolus was still alive. He employed only the finest sculptors, and the resulting monument achieved lasting fame.

Mausolus was the ruler of the kingdom of Caria, a part of the Persian empire that functioned almost as an independent state, and from 377 to 353 BC his ambitious building projects established Halicarnassus as a great city on the Aegean Sea. A Greek architect named Pytheos is credited with designing the Mausoleum, and after Mausolus's death in 353 BC, work was supervised by Artemisia, his wife and successor as ruler. Artemisia herself died before the memorial was finished, but the workers were determined to complete it as a permanent reminder of their remarkable skill. Although it was later destroyed, archaeologists have uncovered many of the Mausoleum's secrets. Halicarnassus was renamed Bodrum, and a museum there now houses some of the tomb's remains.

PLAN OF HALICARNASSUS

Halicarnassus was a magnificent city, surrounded by a 7-km (4.3-mile) wall with gates. The city's landmarks included the Temple of Mars, an amphitheatre that was used for popular public entertainments, and a palace where Mausolus lived with his family and courtiers. The Mausoleum was built on the city's main street, near the market place, emphasizing Mausolus's importance as the founder of Halicarnassus.

Barracks

Palace

Mausoleum   Amphitheatre

City wall / Temple of Mars

A 6-m (20-ft) tall statue of a four-horse chariot sat on top of the roof. Double life size, it was carved in marble and had bronze bits and bridles covered in gold. The chariot was "driven" by a statue of Mausolus.

Around the base of the chariot, a decorative band, called a frieze, showed a fight between Greeks and centaurs, who were part human and part horse.

A series of steps formed a 7-m (22-ft) high pyramid roof made of white marble. Archaeologists have calculated that each of these steps would have been 30 cm (12 in) high.

At the base of the roof, a frieze showed a chariot race. It probably related to four-horse chariot competitions that took place at the funeral of Mausolus.

A frieze, showing Greeks and Amazons, ran around the top of the podium (the structure supporting the columns). The Amazons were a mythical race of warrior women.

BLACK SEA

Ankara

TURKEY

HALICARNASSUS

MEDITERRANEAN SEA

The marble lions around the base of the roof may have been arranged in a line. They were probably intended as guardians to ward off evil.

Marble columns standing 12 m (38 ft) high supported the roof. Spiral ornaments called volutes decorated the tops of these columns, which were made in the Ionic style.

Statues of Mausolus's family stood between the columns. Two giant statues of a man and a woman have survived and are now in the British Museum in London. Some people believe that they represent Mausolus and Artemisia.

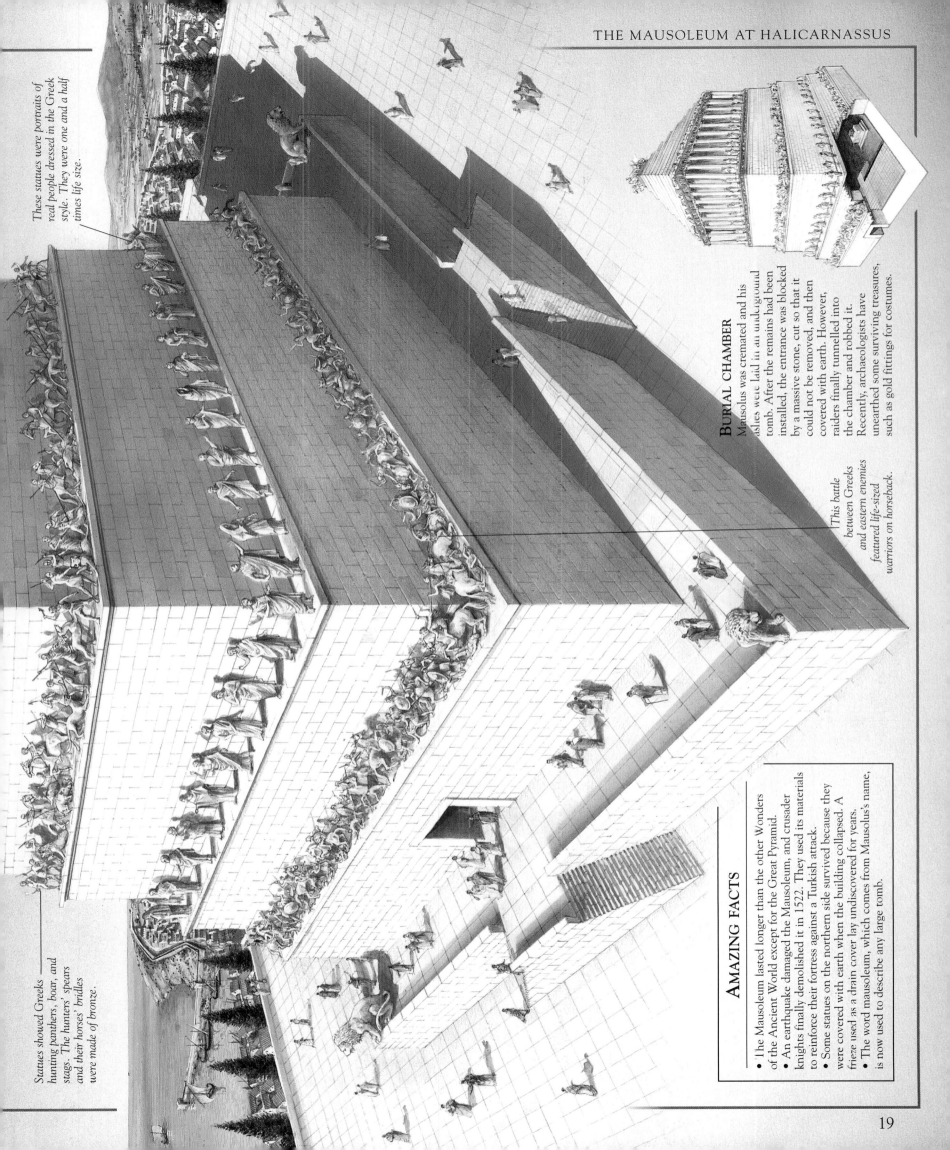

These statues were portraits of real people dressed in the Greek style. They were one and a half times life size.

Statues showed Greeks hunting panthers, boar, and stags. The hunters' spears and their horses' bridles were made of bronze.

BURIAL CHAMBER

Mausolus was cremated and his ashes were laid in an underground tomb. After the remains had been installed, the entrance was blocked by a massive stone, cut so that it could not be removed, and then covered with earth. However, raiders finally tunnelled into the chamber and robbed it. Recently, archaeologists have unearthed some surviving treasures, such as gold fittings for costumes.

This battle between Greeks and eastern enemies featured life-sized warriors on horseback.

AMAZING FACTS

• The Mausoleum lasted longer than the other Wonders of the Ancient World except for the Great Pyramid.
• An earthquake damaged the Mausoleum, and crusader knights finally demolished it in 1522. They used its materials to reinforce their fortress against a Turkish attack.
• Some statues on the northern side survived because they were covered with earth when the building collapsed. A frieze used as a drain cover lay undiscovered for years.
• The word mausoleum, which comes from Mausolus's name, is now used to describe any large tomb.

WORKING WITH STONE

ACCORDING TO THE HISTORIAN PLINY, the stonemasons who laboured on the Mausoleum decided to stay and finish the work without pay after the death of Artemisia. This was because they believed that the monument was "at once a memorial of their own fame and of the sculptor's art". Although much of the structure has now sadly been destroyed or stolen for building materials, enough has been discovered for experts to be fairly certain of its original appearance.

The core of the Mausoleum was built from soft, green lava stone, the blocks measuring about 90 cm (35 in) square and 30 cm (12 in) thick. Large pieces of marble formed its outer surface, and the statues were also carved from marble. Some parts of the tomb were finished with blue limestone as a contrast to the remaining white marble blocks, and the ceiling within the sets of columns was decorated with lifelike carvings showing the Greek hero Theseus.

BODRUM CASTLE

In the modern town of Bodrum, blocks from the Mausoleum can be seen in the walls of the castle erected by crusader knights. The Knights Hospitallers arrived in the early 15th century, and in 1494 they began to take the Mausoleum apart, using its beautifully finished stone to strengthen their castle against a threatened Turkish attack.

Massive marble slabs were quarried nearby, then levered and tied onto oxen carts to be dragged to the site.

AMAZON FRIEZE

Visitors to the Mausoleum marvelled at the quality of the work, in particular the statues and friezes. The Amazon frieze running around the top of the podium (the main structure on which the columns rested) measured 116 m (381 ft) in length. The Knights Hospitallers built slabs of it into their castle wall, which were later removed to Britain.

The frieze represented the triumph of Greek civilization over barbarians from the east. Here, Greek soldiers slay the Queen of the Amazons in two-against-one combat.

SCULPTURE

Pliny's account of the monument states that the statues of people and animals on each of the four sides of the Mausoleum were entrusted to a different sculptor: Scopas worked on the east side, Bryaxis the north, Timotheus the south, and Leochares the west. Above all, it was the beauty of these statues that led to the structure's inclusion among the great Wonders of the World less than a century after it was built. There were probably more than 100 larger-than-life statues around the pillars of the Mausoleum, which would have been a startlingly new idea at the time.

For the first stage in the sculpture, an artist drew the outline of the subject on the marble, in this case a gigantic horse.

The foreman organized the work in minute detail to ensure that it was carried out on time and according to plan. He kept a close eye on the carving of the figures to make sure that they were of the highest quality.

Using hammers and chisels, the sculptors slowly chipped away at the stone. The rough outline of a horse and rider began to rise out of the single block.

The Greek warriors wear plumed helmets and carry shields and swords.

FUNERAL

In Halicarnassus at this time, when someone died, their body was usually cremated (burned). A priest conducted Mausolus's funeral, which took place on the terrace around the Mausoleum. Important people attended, including a representative from the Persian imperial court. Bearers brought a gilded casket in which the ashes and bones of Mausolus were placed for burial.

Twelve slabs showing the battle between the Greeks and the Amazons, together with other sculptures taken from the Mausoleum, are now preserved in the British Museum in London, UK.

The invention of the pulley system around 400 BC is credited to the Greek scientist Archytas of Tarentum. The block and tackle enabled heavy loads to be lifted slowly into place.

The Amazons wear elegant, draped costumes.

Bit by bit, the artist's design took shape.

Skilled workers finally attached bronze parts to the statues, such as a spear for the warrior and the horse's bridle.

Sculptors used powdered quartz and large pebbles to polish the statues and bring out the beauty of the marble.

Stonemasons "dressed" the blocks for the walls, carefully fashioning them to fit perfectly. It took 160,000 of these blocks to build the Mausoleum.

TREMENDOUS TOMBS

THE LASTING WONDER of ancient tombs such as the Mausoleum at Halicarnassus has inspired people from many different cultures to build impressive memorials to their dead. Among wealthy societies with well-developed architectural and artistic skills, the results of their efforts are among the finest structures ever created. The tombs of many great kings and emperors – and, in the case of the Taj Mahal, their wives – have survived. They provide us with information about the societies that honoured their leaders so much that they laboured for years and spent vast fortunes to preserve their memories. The tombs shown here are constructed in a wide variety of styles, and each one is remarkable in its own way.

NAPOLEON'S TOMB

Having conquered much of Europe, Napoleon died in 1821 while exiled on the South Atlantic island of St Helena. His remains were later returned to France, where a magnificent tomb was built for him in the Dôme church of Les Invalides in Paris. In 1861, Napoleon's remains were moved to the tomb, around which the names of his military victories are inscribed. His body was placed in six coffins, one inside the other: the innermost of tinplated iron, the second of mahogany, the third and fourth of lead, the fifth of ebony, and the last of oak. The tomb is now surrounded by those of other French military heroes.

The front of the ship was made to resemble a serpent's head.

The ship is 21.5 m (70 ft 6 in) long and 5 m (16 ft) wide.

Wood, metal, leather, and even woollen cloth were all preserved in the ground under a mound of blue clay, which protected the ship and its contents.

THE TOMB OF NINTOKU

After the Great Pyramid and the Terracotta Warriors, this tomb in Osaka, Japan, is the largest in the world. Believed to be the tomb of the 4th-century emperor Nintoku, it is 486 m (1,594 ft) long and 35 m (115 ft) high and consists of a gigantic keyhole-shaped mound surrounded by three moats. The Emperor would have been buried in the middle, with access via a shaft, and the grave would have been sealed afterwards. Archaeologists excavated the mound in the 19th century, and discovered treasures including gold-plated armour, a helmet, and a sword inside a sarcophagus (stone coffin).

The terracotta soldiers are arranged in ranks, just as in a real army.

THE OSEBERG BURIAL SHIP

Considered the finest of all Viking burial ships, the Oseberg longship was found in 1903. It had been preserved in clay about 113 km (70 miles) south of Oslo, Norway. After it was unearthed, its fragments were treated with preservative and reassembled. Made of oak, the ship had oars for 30 men, but was probably not designed to go to sea. Built around AD 820, it became the burial chamber of a princess and her servant, who were buried with the goods they would need in the afterlife, including cooking pots and a bed.

THE TERRACOTTA WARRIORS

In 1974, workers digging near Xian, in north-west China, stumbled on one of the great archaeological finds of the 20th century: a pit containing a huge army of warriors made of terracotta (hardened clay). They were discovered to be the guardians of the tomb of the first Chinese emperor, Qin Shi Huangdi (259–210 BC). There are more than 6,000 life-sized soldiers in the first pit and even more in two pits that have since been uncovered. They are dressed in a variety of armour and are part of a much larger site. The Emperor's tomb has not yet been explored, but it is believed to lie in an underground palace.

Tutankhamun's mummy wore a beautiful gold mask made to look like the King's face.

TUTANKHAMUN'S TOMB

Tutankhamun was king of Egypt from the age of nine until his death at 18 in 1327 BC. His tomb in the Valley of the Kings, Thebes, was buried under rubble from the building of the tomb of Ramses VI, and so was not disturbed by robbers. When British archaeologist Howard Carter found it in 1922, the tomb was intact and contained some of the best examples of Egyptian art. The mummy of "King Tut" lay within three coffins, the innermost of solid gold and the outer coffins of gilded wood.

The four shrines containing the coffins fitted one inside the other. They were covered in gold and engraved with religious writings and symbols.

The central building, where the Emperor and his wife are buried, is crowned with a massive dome.

The sandstone from which the Treasury is carved is so soft that chips can easily be knocked out of the rock.

"TREASURY OF PHARAOH"

A narrow gap between rocks leads to the Khasneh, or "Treasury of Pharaoh", an unfinished tomb at Petra in south-west Jordan. The Treasury is part of a group of tombs built in the 3rd century by the Nabataean people, who were later conquered by the Romans. The pink sandstone structure is 27 m (90 ft) wide and 40 m (130 ft) tall and was carved out of a sheer rock-face. The Treasury later served as a Christian church and was used by the crusaders as a stronghold. It was rediscovered by the Swiss explorer John Burckhardt in 1812.

THE TAJ MAHAL

India's most famous monument, the Taj Mahal, is situated on the banks of the River Jumna near Agra. It was built as a tomb to commemorate Mumtaz Mahal, the favourite wife of the Mogul emperor Shah Jehan, and now houses both of their bodies. The Emperor employed leading architects to build the mausoleum with the help of more than 20,000 workers, and it was completed in 1643. Because human images are forbidden in Islamic art, the marble used to decorate the tomb is patterned with plant designs. Some of the Taj Mahal's treasures have been stolen, but it has been lovingly restored.

The white marble is decorated with religious verses in black marble and inlaid with jewels.

Four identical circular minarets, like those of a mosque, stand at the corners of the site.

A marble platform raises the Taj Mahal above the river's flood plain.

THE HANGING GARDENS OF BABYLON

THE HANGING GARDENS OF BABYLON have captured the imagination of the world for more than 2,000 years, but astonishingly there is no evidence that they ever existed. Ancient accounts of the city of Babylon (in present-day Iraq) do not mention the Gardens, and although archaeologists have excavated the ancient city, no remains of the Gardens have ever been found.

According to tradition, the Gardens were built by King Nebuchadnezzar II. Historical records state that Nebuchadnezzar reigned from 605 to 562 BC, that he founded the Babylonian Empire, and then glorified the city of Babylon. Legend says that this powerful ruler decided to build the Hanging Gardens as a beautiful gift for his queen, Amytis.

The city was abandoned in 539 BC after being conquered by the Persians, and now all that is left of the Gardens are the remarkable tales of their existence. However, the remains of similar gardens have been found nearby, and archaeologists have pieced together a picture of how they might have looked.

Many of Babylon's buildings featured distinctive blue glazed bricks.

AN EARTHLY PARADISE

It is said that Nebuchadnezzar built the Hanging Gardens because Amytis was unhappy in her husband's desert kingdom. The lush plants would have reminded Amytis of the rich mountain landscape of her home country of Media in what is now Iran. In this artificial paradise the royal couple could stroll, rest, and dine with their courtiers.

Date palm

Queen Amytis is enjoying the scent of an exotic flower while a servant fans her to keep cool. She might also have sampled fresh dates, pomegranates, and other fruits cultivated in the Gardens.

King Nebuchadnezzar II relaxes in the Gardens, protected from the blazing sun by a canopy. Ancient carvings show rulers beneath such awnings, the forerunners of today's garden parasols.

Pomegranate tree

Cypress

Fig tree

Maintaining the Gardens by tilling the soil, planting, watering, hoeing, and pruning would have given employment to hundreds of slaves.

Following his military conquests, the King would have had many enemies, and so would be surrounded by well-armed men.

No one knows for sure what plants were grown, but in his royal gardens at nearby Nimrud, King Ashurnasirpal II (883–859 BC) grew myrtle, juniper, almonds, dates, olives, nightshade, pomegranates, plums, pears, quinces, figs, and grapes.

Fern

Vine

Aloe plant

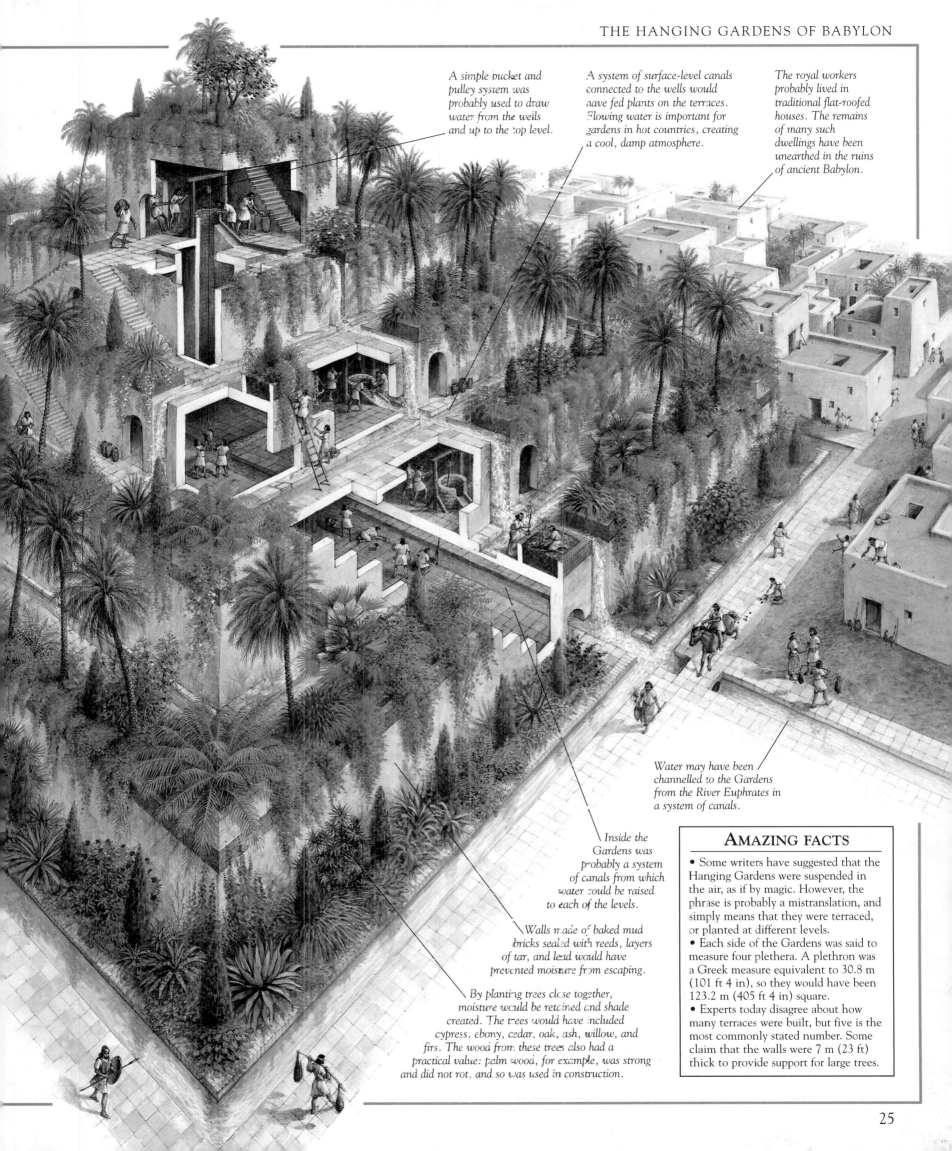

A simple bucket and pulley system was probably used to draw water from the wells and up to the top level.

A system of surface-level canals connected to the wells would have fed plants on the terraces. Flowing water is important for gardens in hot countries, creating a cool, damp atmosphere.

The royal workers probably lived in traditional flat-roofed houses. The remains of many such dwellings have been unearthed in the ruins of ancient Babylon.

Water may have been channelled to the Gardens from the River Euphrates in a system of canals.

Inside the Gardens was probably a system of canals from which water could be raised to each of the levels.

Walls made of baked mud bricks sealed with reeds, layers of tar, and lead would have prevented moisture from escaping.

By planting trees close together, moisture would be retained and shade created. The trees would have included cypress, ebony, cedar, oak, ash, willow, and firs. The wood from these trees also had a practical value: palm wood, for example, was strong and did not rot, and so was used in construction.

AMAZING FACTS

• Some writers have suggested that the Hanging Gardens were suspended in the air, as if by magic. However, the phrase is probably a mistranslation, and simply means that they were terraced, or planted at different levels.

• Each side of the Gardens was said to measure four plethera. A plethron was a Greek measure equivalent to 30.8 m (101 ft 4 in), so they would have been 123.2 m (405 ft 4 in) square.

• Experts today disagree about how many terraces were built, but five is the most commonly stated number. Some claim that the walls were 7 m (23 ft) thick to provide support for large trees.

25

SPLENDOURS OF BABYLON

UNDER THE MIGHTY WARRIOR NEBUCHADNEZZAR II, Babylon became the largest city in the world, covering an area of up to 10 sq km (3.8 sq miles). The capital of a great empire, Babylon was situated on the River Euphrates about 88 km (55 miles) south of Baghdad, near the modern town of Al-Hillah, Iraq. Nebuchadnezzar, who appears in the Bible, took many prisoners to Babylon to work on a building programme that made the city famous for its architecture and as a centre of learning and religion.

The Persians later conquered the city and destroyed many of its buildings. In 331 BC, Alexander the Great seized power in Babylon, and died there in 323 BC. Excavations from 1899 to 1917 revealed the layout of the ancient city and unearthed many treasures. Since the 1950s, many fine pieces of architecture have been restored.

Processional Way
City wall
Hanging Gardens
Ishtar Gate
Moat
Ziggurat of Marduk
River Euphrates
Southern Palace
Northern Palace

PLAN OF CENTRAL BABYLON

The moat outside the city walls provided additional defence and may have been fed by a reservoir used to control the flow of water. Soldiers stood guard on the bridges that ran across the moat in order to protect the wealthiest parts of Babylon.

The great double walls that surrounded the city were begun by King Nabopolassar and finished by Nebuchadnezzar II. They were so impressive that they were once regarded as a Wonder of the World. The Greek writer Antipater even described how chariots could race along them.

The Ishtar Gate controlled the most important route into the city and was dedicated to Ishtar, the Babylonian goddess of love and war. It measured more than 12 m (38 ft) high and was built during the reign of Nebuchadnezzar II using mud bricks.

On the Ishtar Gate there were 13 alternate rows of glazed bricks decorated with as many as 575 images of dragons and bulls.

The Processional Way led from the Ishtar Gate and ran for more than 800 m (half a mile). Images of lions lined the route.

ISHTAR GATE DRAGON

A "dragon" with a forked tongue is the main animal associated with the god Marduk. This relief (a picture made of bricks), known as the Dragon of Marduk, shows a monster with a reptile's scaly body, a snake's head, cat-like front paws, the rear feet of a bird, and the tail of a scorpion. Once part of the Ishtar Gate, it is made of glazed bricks on a blue background.

MAKING THE BRICKS

Babylon was known as the city of brick. The first sun-dried mud bricks were produced around 4000 BC. At about this time, the Mesopotamian city of Ur had the first known brick arch. Bricks were easy to build with because they were all the same size. They could be set in regular layers to build walls.

Clay silt was taken from the river and mixed with water in shallow pits. About 60 kg (132 lb) of straw per 100 bricks was added to strengthen them.

The mixture was shaped into bricks by pressing it into moulds. Bricks were left to dry in the sun, then tapped out and joined together with mortar.

If the bricks were to be glazed for palace walls they were put into wood-fired kilns and baked. Some of these glazed bricks have survived.

Some archaeologists have proposed a site for the Hanging Gardens between the Processional Way and the Southern Palace.

In Nebuchadnezzar's reign, the Northern Palace was right next to a museum housing important inscriptions.

This temple, called a ziggurat, was dedicated to the god Marduk and probably had seven stages reaching a height of 91 m (300 ft). Some people believe that it inspired the Biblical story of the Tower of Babel.

A temple made of blue glazed bricks was built at the top.

There were two palaces in the city. The Southern Palace was probably even more spectacular than the Northern Palace.

The River Euphrates flowed through the city, providing the water supply, transport, and irrigation for crops and gardens.

WONDERS OF ENTERTAINMENT

The Colosseum has been partially restored and is still an impressive sight today.

SINCE ANCIENT TIMES, people have created buildings for entertainment. From pleasure gardens, such as the Hanging Gardens of Babylon, to sporting and cultural centres and theatres, these structures have catered to our need to express ourselves, and to witness events that stimulate our senses. Every age has different ideas of entertainment: in the Roman empire, the often cruel spectacle of gladiators fighting and battles between wild animals took place in venues such as the Colosseum. When plays became a popular art form, buildings like the Globe Theatre were erected, while in modern times, film-making, art galleries, and sports arenas have given rise to yet more original structures. In most of these, the public attended as spectators, but as people have become more involved as participants, so theme and amusement parks offering more exciting experiences have attracted huge numbers of visitors.

THE COLOSSEUM

Crowds once gathered in this huge amphitheatre in Rome, Italy, to watch bloody gladiator contests and fights between wild animals. The Colosseum was built during the reign of Emperor Vespasian and opened in AD 80 with games that lasted for 100 days. It was made of stone and concrete and, unlike many amphitheatres, it was not built into a hillside for support. Although it was damaged by earthquakes and plundered for building materials in the 15th century, the main structure has survived for almost 2,000 years.

WALT DISNEY WORLD

The largest entertainment complex on Earth, Walt Disney World in Florida, USA, plays host to more than 15 million people every year. For many families, their visit is like a dream come true. The Magic Kingdom with its fairy-tale castle is where children of all ages can meet their favourite Disney characters. Visitors can try the thrilling rides and also explore Epcot, where the attractions include a series of futuristic exhibits and a slice of life from many different countries. Finally, film fans can watch top-quality shows at the Disney-MGM Studios.

Visitors can watch the re-enactment of a scary scene from the film Jaws.

UNIVERSAL STUDIOS

Feature films are now among the most popular forms of entertainment, and the movie industry has grown into a multi-million dollar business centred around Hollywood, Los Angeles, USA. Universal Studios were set up in 1915 and later became the world's largest film and TV studio. When it opened to the public in 1964, visitors could only tour certain sets, but increasing demand led to the building of special rides. Today's visitors can experience special effects including earthquakes and flash floods and watch re-enacted scenes from popular films.

THE SYDNEY OLYMPIC STADIUM

Work on the Sydney Olympic Stadium and the Olympic village was completed in 1999, well ahead of the Olympic Games in 2000. The Stadium will be used for athletics events and for the finals of the soccer competition. This spectacular arena features state-of-the-art electronic scoreboards and giant video screens. Constructed at a cost of £272 million, with seating for 110,000 people, it is the largest Olympic stadium ever built. After the Games, its capacity will be reduced, and there will be 60,000 seats under cover. The Stadium will then be used for concerts and exhibitions as well as other sporting events.

LONGLEAT MAZE

Mazes have fascinated people for thousands of years – labyrinths in Greece have been dated to around 1200 BC. The world's longest hedge maze is this one, designed by Greg Bright at Longleat House in Wiltshire, UK. Opened to the public in 1978, it contains more than 16,000 yew plants, along with six wooden bridges. It originally covered a rectangle measuring 116 x 57 m (381 x 187 ft), with a total of 2.7 km (1.7 miles) of paths, but it has recently been extended. The maze is in two sections and takes about an hour and a half to complete, allowing plenty of time for wrong turns and getting lost.

This aerial view near the middle of the puzzle shows two of the maze's bridges.

THE POMPIDOU CENTRE

The inside-out design of the Pompidou Centre amazes visitors with its escalators, pipes, and structural supports on the outside. It is one of the most visited arts centres in the world, attracting 25,000 people per day. Built between 1972 and 1976, the Centre brings together a wide range of cultural activities under one roof, including a museum of modern art, exhibitions, libraries, cinemas, and study centres. When it was first completed, its unusual design was very controversial, but it is now widely appreciated. The blue pipes are for air, the green ones are for water, and the yellow ones are for electricity lines. Routes used by people are colour-coded red.

For many people the structure of the Pompidou Centre makes it look like an ocean liner or even a factory.

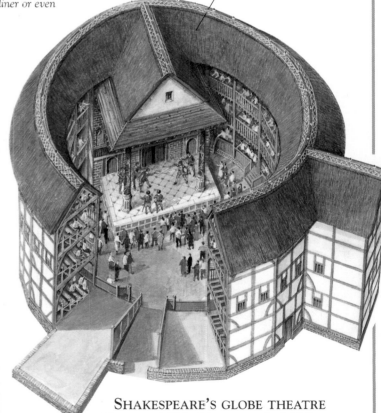

The reconstructed Globe Theatre is 30 m (98 ft) in diameter and 14 m (45 ft) high.

SHAKESPEARE'S GLOBE THEATRE

The original Globe Theatre, in which William Shakespeare's plays were performed, stood by the River Thames in London, UK, and was completed in 1599. Its thatched roof later caught fire, and the Globe was pulled down in 1644. In 1970, an American film actor and director named Sam Wanamaker put forward the idea of building a replica theatre using traditional materials. The new building finally opened in 1997 as Shakespeare's Globe Theatre, and it is now very popular with theatre-goers. It has an open thatched roof and holds an audience of 1,600, with 700 people known in Shakespeare's day as "groundlings", standing near the stage.

THE COLOSSUS OF RHODES

IN 304 BC, THE PEOPLE OF RHODES were saved from a terrible siege. This was a great cause for celebration, as it was the third siege to threaten the island in only 30 years. The people were so grateful that they decided to build a huge statue of the Sun god, Helios, who was also the patron god of their island. The statue was funded by the sale of military equipment left behind by Demetrius Poliorcetes, who, with an army of 40,000 troops, had mounted a long and determined attack on the capital city.

Construction of the 32-m (106-ft) bronze statue, which became known as the Colossus, began in 292 BC and lasted for a total of 12 years. The statue stood on a marble base beside the harbour and was built using bronze sheets and shaped sections of bronze over an iron framework. Despite the best efforts of its sculptor, Chares of Lindos, the Colossus remained standing for less than 60 years, making it the shortest-lived monument of all the Seven Wonders. Sadly, it was destroyed in a powerful earthquake in 226 BC, when it broke at the knees and crashed to the ground in pieces. The shattered remains were left where they fell until AD 654, when Arabs who had invaded Rhodes sold the bronze pieces to a merchant from Syria, who carried them away on the backs of 900 camels. Not a single trace of the Colossus survives today.

The statue of the Sun god probably had a fiery crown of sunbeams on its head.

Historians believe that Chares modelled the head of the Colossus on that of Alexander the Great, who was shown as a powerful and godlike hero.

Chares's teacher Lysippus encouraged his students to adopt a lifelike style for their sculptures that implied strength and vigorous movement.

A 14th-century Italian pilgrim called de Martoni thought that the Colossus held a blazing torch as a guiding light for ships.

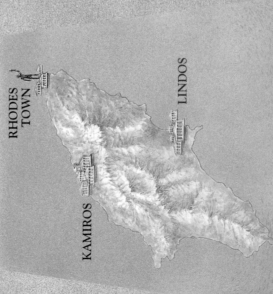

GREECE

Athens

RHODES TOWN

MEDITERRANEAN SEA

MAP OF RHODES

Rhodes is the largest of the Greek Dodecanese islands and lies about 19 km (12 miles) off the Turkish coast. The harbour of the capital city, which is also called Rhodes, is believed to have been the location of the Colossus, but no one knows for certain exactly where it stood. This map shows the island's three principal towns at the time when the Colossus was first built.

KAMIROS

RHODES TOWN

LINDOS

This temple was dedicated to the god Helios. Some people believe that the Colossus was actually situated here and not beside the sea.

Each finger was said to be so big that a person's arms could not encircle it.

Some surviving images of the Colossus show him naked, others with a loincloth or cloak.

Once considered among the world's finest cities, Rhodes was an important trading centre with a busy harbour.

A strong 15-km (9-mile) wall protected the city. It was surrounded by a ditch so that attackers had to use siege towers for any attempt to scale it.

MAKING THE COLOSSUS

MINING FOR COPPER

People have used copper since ancient times – it was the first metal to be widely mined, and has long been important in the manufacture of coins. Most copper comes from beneath ground level, and the Greeks imported their supplies from Cyprus. Mining in ancient times was a hard labour, and frequent cave-ins resulted in many deaths. Shafts could be more than 12 m (40 ft) deep, and miners worked in tunnels with ceilings so low that it was impossible for them to stand up.

A furnace was used for extracting the copper.

The copper ore was winched to the surface in baskets.

A shaft led to the mining area, and workers used long ladders to reach the tunnels.

Miners worked long hours in cramped conditions, using pick axes to hack away rocks containing ore.

Oil lamps were used to light up the mine. The smoky, airless conditions would have been very uncomfortable.

Wooden pillars supported the walls and roof of the tunnel.

THE ISLAND OF RHODES WAS FAMOUS for its statues, and according to the Roman writer Pliny, the capital city boasted as many as 3,000 examples. Some were carved in stone, and others, like the Colossus, were made of bronze. Although large bronze statues had been made elsewhere, such as Phidias's 12-m (40-ft) high Athene at the Parthenon in Athens, no one had previously tried to create one on the mighty scale of the Colossus.

Around 2500 BC it had been discovered that melting copper with tin created bronze, an alloy (a combination of two or more metals) that is much harder than either metal alone. Bronze is also easier to cast by pouring the molten (liquid) metal into moulds. The ancient Greeks used this alloy for weapons and armour, and it was ideal for making life-size outdoor statues. However, a bronze statue the size of the Colossus would have had to be built in sections. The rounded shapes were probably cast and made to interlock, while the large areas were constructed of panels mounted on an iron framework.

Making bronze requires a temperature of over 1,000° C (1,832° F). The furnace would have been made of bricks lined with clay.

Bellows were invented around 2500 BC. They were used as a pump to increase the flow of air, raising the temperature of the furnace.

After the metal cooled, the specially shaped sections were removed from their moulds. The rough edges of these sections would then be smoothed off and their outer surfaces polished.

MAKING THE BRONZE PLATES

Bronze is stronger than iron and resists being worn away by harsh weather conditions. These qualities make it suited for outdoor statues, especially those near the sea exposed to salty air. When the Colossus was built, it was very difficult to cast statues much larger than life size from a single mould. The only way that workers could construct the Colossus was to assemble it from a range of shaped sections and sheets. One early account claimed that the Colossus included more than 13 tonnes of bronze, but this may be an underestimate. The cast shapes used at the statue's base were made in moulds, and the panels were beaten from thin sheets of metal.

Lumps of copper and blocks of tin, called ingots, were weighed and combined in the right proportion to create bronze. Copper probably made up between 80 and 90 per cent of the bronze alloy used to build the Colossus.

Copper and tin were mixed together to make an alloy. Bronze melts more easily than copper, and flows more freely, so it is ideal for casting. Workers carried the molten metal from the furnace to the mould in a giant iron spoon.

Metal workers poured molten bronze into different moulds to make special shapes and thin sheets of metal. These clay moulds could be re-used or broken apart once the metal had solidified.

A GIANT UNDERTAKING

Starting with a large marble base, the builders of the Colossus assembled the gigantic statue piece by piece. Moulded sections that joined together formed the feet, which were longer than the total height of most other statues. Heavy stone blocks were used to "anchor" the lower parts of the legs, and a sturdy iron framework was built up around them for attaching the thinner hammered plates. Each plate was beaten into shape before being hoisted into position and fixed to the adjoining plates and the iron frame. Gradually the Colossus grew taller, the workers carefully raising and joining the sections to create what was probably the largest bronze statue ever made. Finally, the workers would have polished the surface of the Colossus with abrasives until it gleamed in the sunlight.

The thinner shaped plates were fixed onto the iron frame with rivets made of copper. Rivets are short pegs that are passed through holes and then hammered over to keep them firmly in place sealing the sections from the effects of the weather.

Some experts believe that after the first stages were built, workers would have used an earth ramp to raise the materials to the higher parts, removing it when the statue was completed.

Many of the labourers would have been slaves, who worked alongside skilled craftsmen. These slaves received no payment and were often used for exhausting tasks.

The heavy castings were probably fitted together with pegs slotting into holes, like toy building blocks, but on a massive scale.

Heavy blocks of stone were used to stabilize the lower portions of the Colossus. These blocks were encased by the iron framework and bronze covering.

The Colossus was said to have contained an iron framework weighing more than 8 tonnes. This was tied into the stone blocks and used to attach the bronze sections.

Bronze is more difficult to shape by beating than pure copper. Hammering changes the structure of metals, causing them to harden. Annealing (heating) hammered bronze at a temperature of 426° to 537° C (800° to 1,000° F) softens it again, allowing it to be steadily worked into shape.

The statue's toes would have been made of large cast sections to achieve perfect curves and to add weight and stability to the base of the statue.

Bronze is a very heavy material; a cube with 30 cm (12 in) sides weighs 248 kg (548 lb) — as much as three adult men. Teams of slaves would have been used to haul the pieces into position.

The Colossus was assembled on a base of white marble. Starting with its feet and legs, it steadily grew until it reached a towering height of 105 Grecian feet, the equivalent of 32 m (106 ft).

Chares of Lindos supervised work on his great construction. He probably made small models and scaled these up to get the proportions of the giant statue correct.

MIGHTY MONUMENTS

SINCE EARLY TIMES, humans have made memorials to pay tribute to the people or the virtues they most admired, often by creating dramatic larger-than-life statues, such as the Colossus of Rhodes. Monuments from the ancient world are especially impressive because of the technical difficulties that their creators often faced, but in modern times new construction methods and materials – including the use of explosives, powerful drills, and cranes – have enabled sculptors to make even more extraordinary statues. Here are some outstanding examples dating from the Roman period to the present day. They include the largest sculptures ever made and works of genius and single-minded determination that are among the most amazing and the most famous statues in the world.

The steel sword is 29 m (95 ft) long and weighs 14 tonnes.

MOTHERLAND

Like the Colossus of Rhodes, Motherland was built to commemorate a military victory. It is the world's tallest free-standing statue and represents Mother Russia calling upon her children to defend their country. From the base of her pedestal to the tip of her sword, Motherland is 82 m (270 ft) tall. Designed by Yevgeni Vuchetich, the concrete and steel statue stands in Volgograd, Russia, and was completed in 1967 as a memorial of the Russian defeat of the German army at the Battle of Stalingrad in 1942–43.

TRAJAN'S COLUMN

This marble column in Rome, Italy, was completed in AD 113 and celebrates the military triumphs of Emperor Trajan. Spiralling up the 38-m (125-ft) structure is a series of detailed scenes that tell the story of the Emperor's campaigns in Dacia (now Romania). A continuous band 1.2 m (4 ft) wide, like a long comic strip, runs for a total of 244 m (800 ft). A staircase inside the monument once took visitors to the top, where a statue of Saint Peter now stands.

Detailed carvings
This part of the Column shows groups of soldiers building a fort and a bridge. The carvings provide vivid glimpses of warfare and scenes of Roman life.

The mythical Thunderbird is usually set high on the pole. The Grand Lord of the Sky Realm, he was said to control lightning.

TOTEM POLE

A traditional art form of the north-west coast of North America, many totem poles are massive structures. As they are at risk from severe weather, some poles have now been preserved in museums. They represent the histories and achievements of native families, often recording dead ancestors, and they include figures of legendary people as well as animals and birds. Contrary to popular belief, totem poles have never been used to ward off evil spirits. This example, topped by a Thunderbird, stands in Stanley Park in Vancouver, Canada. There has been a collection of totem poles there since 1889, and the park is visited by eight million people a year.

People can climb 354 steps to Liberty's crown, which is the highest level open to visitors. The seven spikes represent the world's seven seas and seven continents.

THE STATUE OF LIBERTY

This splendid statue was a gift to the people of the United States of America from the people of France. It has become a symbol of freedom, recognized throughout the world. The Statue of Liberty was designed by the French sculptor Frédéric-Auguste Bartholdi, who used his mother as the model, gradually scaling it up from smaller replicas. It is made of 91 tonnes of copper sheets hammered into shape over a huge iron framework. First erected in Paris in 1884, the Statue was then shipped to New York in 350 pieces. In 1886, it was finally assembled and unveiled for all to see.

The torch's flame was restored in 1986 and is now coated in gold leaf. At night it is illuminated by floodlights.

EASTER ISLAND STONE HEADS

These bizarre statues stand on Easter Island in the Pacific Ocean, apparently keeping watch over the barren landscape. This remote island, which lies 3,700 km (2,300 miles) west of Chile, got its name because the first Europeans to go there arrived on Easter Sunday in 1722. The impressive army of statues, called *moai*, was built by the Easter Islanders in honour of their dead chiefs. The heads were carved from volcanic stone and may have been dragged from quarries on wooden sledges or rollers. They have been dated to around AD 1000–1600, but despite many investigations they remain shrouded in mystery.

There are more than 600 moai, some more than 10 m (33 ft) tall and weighing at least 90 tonnes. The Easter Islanders carved many statues with long heads, whose arms were pressed tightly to their sides.

MOUNT RUSHMORE

This monument in the Black Hills of South Dakota, USA, was once the world's largest portrait sculpture. Mount Rushmore National Memorial consists of four giant heads of US presidents George Washington, Thomas Jefferson, Theodore Roosevelt, and Abraham Lincoln, each about 18 m (60 ft) high. The project began in 1927 when workers, led by sculptor Gutzon Borglum, used dynamite to blast away rock from the granite cliff. Mount Rushmore has become a world famous tourist attraction visited by more than two million people a year.

CRAZY HORSE STATUE

In 1939, US sculptor Korczak Ziolkowski was invited by the Sioux people to create a memorial to their leader, Crazy Horse. Ziolkowski started work in the Black Hills of South Dakota in 1948, blasting away tonnes of rock to make a statue of the chief seated on his horse. The monument is an amazing 172 m (563 ft) high and 195 m (641 ft) long, and because of its huge size a cable car was used to carry tools to carve the head. Since his death in 1982, the sculptor's family have continued to work on the statue, which will take many more years to complete.

THE PHAROS AT ALEXANDRIA

SEEN AT NIGHT, the Pharos of Alexandria would have been an amazing spectacle, shining brightly to warn ships of dangerous underwater rocks. The last-built of the Seven Wonders, this lighthouse was also the most useful. For centuries the Pharos was the highest habitable structure in the world. It stood for nearly 1,700 years and to this day remains the tallest lighthouse ever constructed.

Alexander the Great founded the city of Alexandria in 332 BC. It was originally a tiny fishing village, and many ships were wrecked on nearby offshore rocks. The growing importance of the city meant that a lighthouse was needed to guide ships safely into the port, so around 299 BC Alexander's successor, Ptolemy Soter (305–282 BC), began to build one on a nearby island, called Pharos. It took about 20 years to complete.

Arabs later conquered Alexandria, and as the city declined in importance and the harbour silted up, the Pharos was no longer required. Earthquakes rocked the structure, and it eventually collapsed into the sea.

PRESENT SITE

Many experts believe that the Islamic fortress of Qait Bey stands on the site of the Pharos. The fort, built in 1480 by Sultan Qait Bey, probably includes materials taken from the lighthouse ruins. Other remains of the Pharos toppled into the sea in devastating earthquakes.

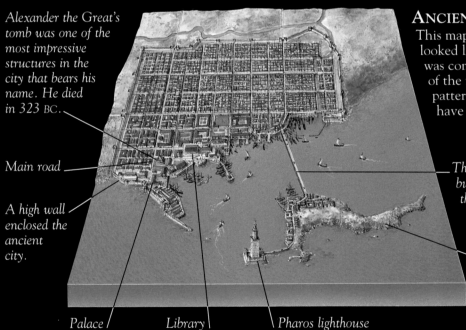

Alexander the Great's tomb was one of the most impressive structures in the city that bears his name. He died in 323 BC.

Main road

A high wall enclosed the ancient city.

Palace   *Library*   *Pharos lighthouse*

ANCIENT ALEXANDRIA

This map shows what Alexandria looked like soon after the Pharos was completed. The city was one of the first to be built on a grid pattern. Many modern cities have a similar street plan.

The Hepstadion causeway was built to link Pharos island to the mainland.

Pharos island was barren and rocky.

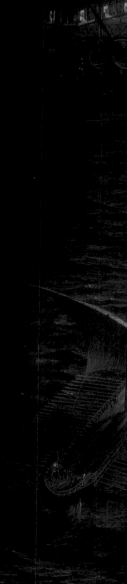

AMAZING FACTS

- The Pharos was not counted among the Seven Wonders of the World until the 6th century AD.
- One writer said that the Pharos towered to "306 fathoms" – taller than the tallest skyscraper.
- According to one source, the Pharos cost "800 talents" of silver to build – nearly £4 million today.

- Some people claimed that the mirror at the top reflected events in Byzantium (Istanbul) 1,250 km (777 miles) away.
- In the 1990s, the French archaeologist Jean-Yves Empereur and his team mapped underwater remains, including statues that may have been part of the Pharos.

A TOWERING ACHIEVEMENT

SOARING TO A HEIGHT of about 124 m (407 ft), the Pharos guided mariners to safety through dangerous rocks for many centuries. Incredibly, it was taller than the tallest lighthouse in the world today – a 106-m (348-ft) structure in Yokohama, Japan. The Pharos became the model for later lighthouses all over the world, and it was unquestionably one of the greatest engineering feats of ancient times.

The lighthouse bore the inscription "Sostratus, the son of Dexiphanes, the Cnidian, dedicated this to the Saviour Gods on behalf of those who sail the seas", and it became the subject of many legends. According to one source, the mirror at the top was used to focus the sunlight onto invading galleys to set them alight. Information about its appearance comes from a variety of sources, including pictures on ancient coins and mosaics, studies of similar structures that have survived, and travellers' accounts. One of these accounts was written by Ibn al Shaikh, an Arab who visited Alexandria in 1165–66. He carefully measured the remarkable lighthouse using a length of string.

The mirror may have been used as a heliograph – a signalling device that reflects the Sun's rays. Perhaps it sent messages to Alexandria about incoming ships.

The Jewish historian Josephus (c.AD 37–100) calculated that the light could be seen from a distance of 300 stadia – 56 km (35 miles).

This 6-m (20-ft) high statue was once thought to represent Poseidon, god of the sea. It is now believed to have been Zeus Soter. (Soter means "Saviour"). According to the writer Strabo, the statue's finger somehow pointed to the Sun, following as it rose, and lowering as it set.

The mirror for signalling may have been designed by the Greek scientist Archimedes (c.287–212 BC). It was made of highly polished bronze.

A system of ropes and pulleys was used to raise fuel to the fire chamber.

The top tier was probably cylindrical and 21 m (69 ft) high.

Ramps were used instead of stairs so that the animals could climb up.

The middle tier was probably octagonal (eight-sided), rising to 30 m (98 ft).

Statues of Tritons – Greek sea gods – kept watch over the harbour.

THE FIRE CHAMBER

Pictures of other lighthouses of the period show flames licking out from their topmost storey. The fire chamber had no outer walls, which allowed the air to circulate and kept the torches alight. A great deal of fuel was needed to keep the flames burning. Wood was scarce in Alexandria, so bundles of pine branches were imported by barge. During its long lifetime, the Pharos would have burnt the wood of over a million trees.

BEASTS OF BURDEN
Horses or mules were stabled in the Pharos. They brought up the fuel needed to keep the fires lit throughout the night and carried away the ashes the next day. This was hard work in the heat of the city, so large numbers of animals would probably have worked in shifts.

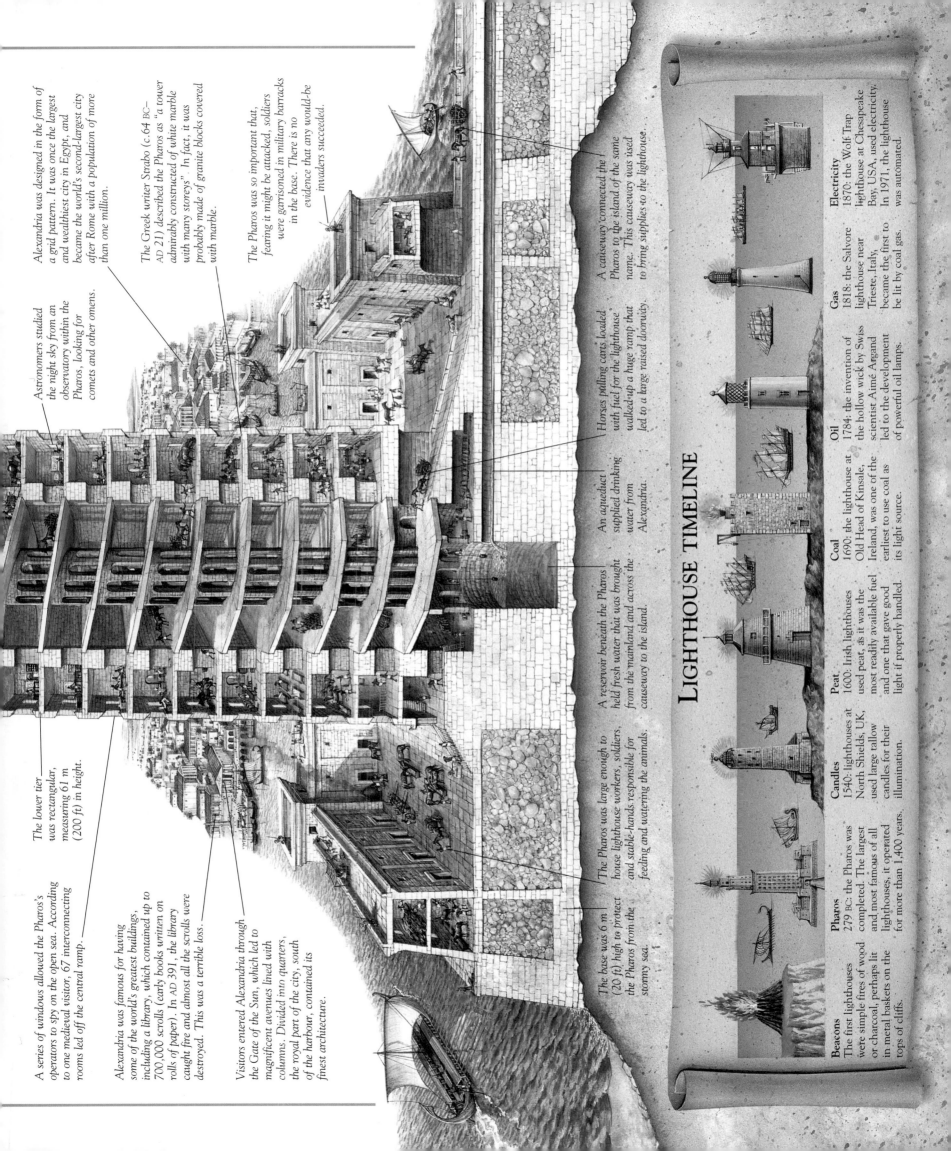

A series of windows allowed the Pharos's operators to spy on the open sea. According to one medieval visitor, 67 interconnecting rooms led off the central ramp.

Alexandria was famous for having some of the world's greatest buildings, including a library, which contained up to 700,000 scrolls (early books written on rolls of paper). In AD 391, the library caught fire and almost all the scrolls were destroyed. This was a terrible loss.

Visitors entered Alexandria through the Gate of the Sun, which led to magnificent avenues lined with columns. Divided into quarters, the royal part of the city, south of the harbour, contained its finest architecture.

The lower tier was rectangular, measuring 61 m (200 ft) in height.

Alexandria was designed in the form of a grid pattern. It was once the largest and wealthiest city in Egypt, and became the world's second-largest city after Rome with a population of more than one million.

Astronomers studied the night sky from an observatory within the Pharos, looking for comets and other omens.

The Greek writer Strabo (c.64 BC–AD 21) described the Pharos as "a tower admirably constructed of white marble with many storeys". In fact, it was probably made of granite blocks covered with marble.

The Pharos was so important that, fearing it might be attacked, soldiers were garrisoned in military barracks in the base. There is no evidence that any would-be invaders succeeded.

A causeway connected the Pharos to the island of the same name. This causeway was used to bring supplies to the lighthouse.

Horses pulling carts loaded with fuel for the lighthouse walked up a huge ramp that led to a large raised doorway.

An aqueduct supplied drinking water from Alexandria.

A reservoir beneath the Pharos held fresh water that was brought from the mainland and across the causeway to the island.

The Pharos was large enough to house lighthouse workers, soldiers, and stable-hands responsible for feeding and watering the animals.

The base was 6 m (20 ft) high to protect the Pharos from the stormy sea.

LIGHTHOUSE TIMELINE

Beacons
The first lighthouses were simple fires of wood or charcoal, perhaps lit in metal baskets on the tops of cliffs.

Pharos
279 BC: the Pharos was completed. The largest and most famous of all lighthouses, it operated for more than 1,400 years.

Candles
1540: lighthouses at North Shields, UK, used large tallow candles for their illumination.

Peat
1600: Irish lighthouses used peat, as it was the most readily available fuel and one that gave good light if properly handled.

Coal
1690: the lighthouse at Old Head of Kinsale, Ireland, was one of the earliest to use coal as its light source.

Oil
1784: the invention of the hollow wick by Swiss scientist Aimé Argand led to the development of powerful oil lamps.

Gas
1818: the Salvore lighthouse near Trieste, Italy, became the first to be lit by coal gas.

Electricity
1870: the Wolf Trap lighthouse at Chesapeake Bay, USA, used electricity. In 1971, the lighthouse was automated.

REACHING FOR THE SKY

THE PYRAMIDS OF ANCIENT EGYPT, the great churches of medieval Europe, Asia's towering pagodas, and, of course, the Pharos at Alexandria are all evidence of the human desire to build taller and taller structures. However, up to 100 years ago, the engineering methods and materials available made it almost impossible to construct tall buildings in which people could actually live. The invention of steel-framed buildings and electric lifts first made skyscrapers practical, with Chicago, and then New York, leading the trend ever upwards. Fanciful ideas for mile-high buildings have yet to be realized, but new office buildings and telecommunication towers continue the passion to win the title of "world's tallest building".

BIG BEN

London's most famous landmark, "Big Ben" is actually the name of a 14-tonne bell in St Stephen's Tower, part of the Houses of Parliament. However, "Big Ben" has come to mean the Tower itself. Begun in 1840 and completed in 1859, the elegant Tower is 96 m (316 ft) tall. It contains a clock with four dials 6.8 m (22 ft 6 in) across, at one time the world's largest. The minute hands on each dial are 4.5 m (14 ft) long.

EIFFEL TOWER

One of the world's best-known landmarks, the Eiffel Tower in Paris, France, was built as a temporary structure for the 1889 Universal Exhibition but has never been taken down. Designed by two engineers who worked for Gustave Eiffel, it took 300 steel workers two years, two months, and five days to build. At 300 m (986 ft) it was the world's tallest structure until 1930, when it was overtaken by New York's Chrysler Building. The Tower still attracts five million visitors a year.

CN TOWER

The world's tallest free-standing structure, the CN Tower in Toronto, Canada, measures 553.3 m (1,815 ft 5 in) to the tip of its antenna. The Tower opened in 1976 at a cost of £38 million. First built to improve TV transmissions blocked by other skyscrapers, it has now become a popular tourist attraction. Almost two million people each year visit its Sky Pod level, which houses the world's tallest observatory at 447 m (1,465 ft).

The TV tower was a later addition that took the overall height to 443 m (1,454 ft). The lightning conductor was struck 68 times in the structure's first 10 years.

On a clear day, the view from the 102nd floor is more than 120 km (75 miles).

The spire on top of the building was designed as an airship mooring mast.

Coloured lights illuminate the building at night. They are changed for seasonal celebrations: red, white, and blue on Independence Day, green on St Patrick's Day, and so on.

There are 6,500 windows in total.

On 28 July 1945, a B-25 bomber crashed into the building between the 78th and 79th floors, killing 14 people.

PORCELAIN PAGODA

Nanking (now Nanjing), on the southern bank of the Yangtse Kiang River, was once the capital of China. In around 1412, Emperor Yung-lo built the Porcelain Pagoda there to honour his dead father, Emperor Hung-wu. It was octagonal (eight-sided) in shape, and 79 m (260 ft) tall, with nine storeys. Visitors marvelled at the Pagoda and ascended it to view the city. It was often included in lists of Wonders of the Middle Ages.

On the summit stood an iron rod encircled by iron rings with a gold-plated ball at the top.

White porcelain bricks covered the outer surface.

Green glazed tiles covered the roof of each storey. The tiles were made in the Imperial kilns of Jungdezhen.

Pagodas traditionally had an uneven number of storeys to bring luck. The Porcelain Pagoda had nine storeys and a base.

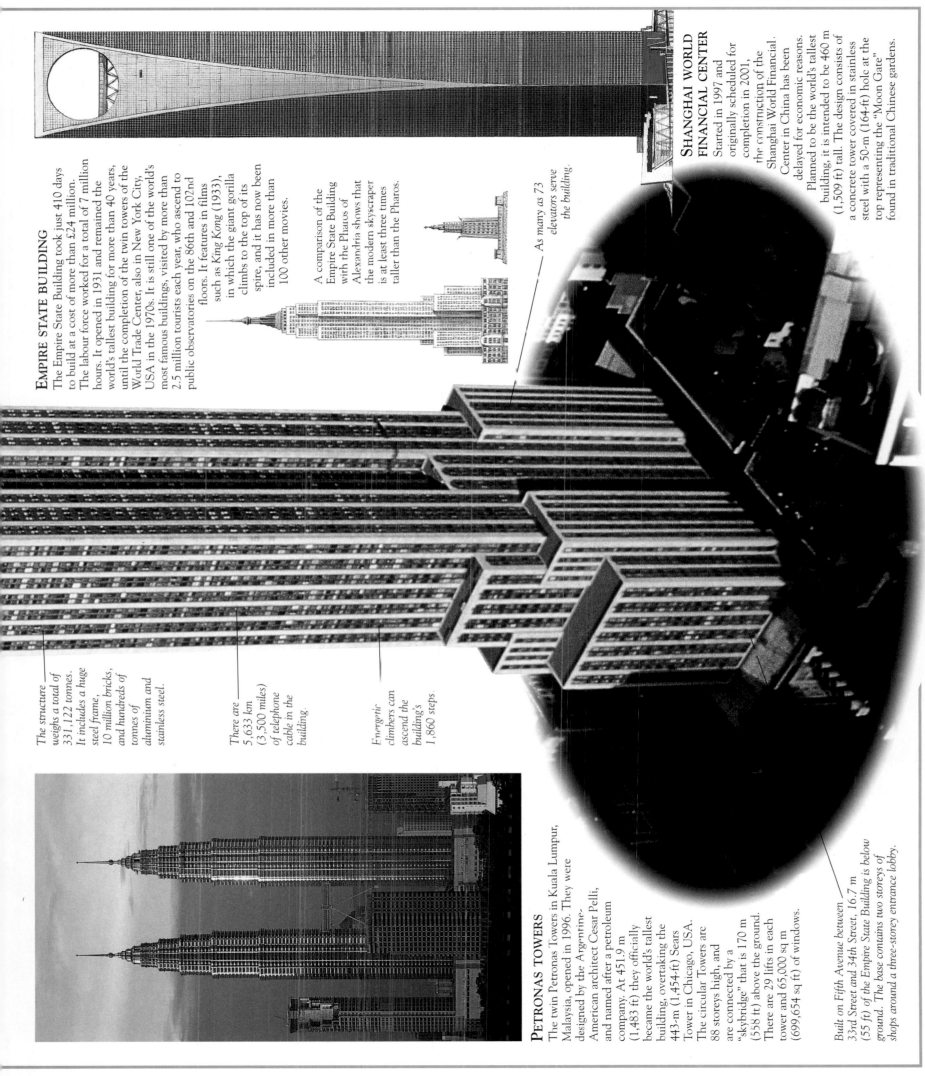

EMPIRE STATE BUILDING

The Empire State Building took just 410 days to build at a cost of more than £24 million. The labour force worked for a total of 7 million hours. It opened in 1931 and remained the world's tallest building for more than 40 years, until the completion of the twin towers of the World Trade Center, also in New York City, USA in the 1970s. It is still one of the world's most famous buildings, visited by more than 2.5 million tourists each year, who ascend to public observatories on the 86th and 102nd floors. It features in films such as *King Kong* (1933), in which the giant gorilla climbs to the top of its spire, and it has now been included in more than 100 other movies.

A comparison of the Empire State Building with the Pharos of Alexandria shows that the modern skyscraper is at least three times taller than the Pharos.

As many as 73 elevators serve the building.

The structure weighs a total of 331,122 tonnes. It includes a huge steel frame, 10 million bricks, and hundreds of tonnes of aluminium and stainless steel.

There are 5,633 km (3,500 miles) of telephone cable in the building.

Energetic climbers can ascend the building's 1,860 steps.

SHANGHAI WORLD FINANCIAL CENTER

Started in 1997 and originally scheduled for completion in 2001, the construction of the Shanghai World Financial Center in China has been delayed for economic reasons. Planned to be the world's tallest building, it is intended to be 460 m (1,509 ft) tall. The design consists of a concrete tower covered in stainless steel with a 50-m (164-ft) hole at the top representing the "Moon Gate" found in traditional Chinese gardens.

PETRONAS TOWERS

The twin Petronas Towers in Kuala Lumpur, Malaysia, opened in 1996. They were designed by the Argentine-American architect Cesar Pelli, and named after a petroleum company. At 451.9 m (1,483 ft) they officially became the world's tallest building, overtaking the 443-m (1,454-ft) Sears Tower in Chicago, USA. The circular Towers are 88 storeys high, and are connected by a "skybridge" that is 170 m (558 ft) above the ground. There are 29 lifts in each tower and 65,000 sq m (699,654 sq ft) of windows.

Built on Fifth Avenue between 33rd Street and 34th Street, 16.7 m (55 ft) of the Empire State Building is below ground. The base contains two storeys of shops around a three-storey entrance lobby.

THE TEMPLE OF ARTEMIS AT EPHESUS

THE FAMOUS TEMPLE OF ARTEMIS, which became one of the Seven Wonders, was not the first temple to be built at Ephesus, but it was certainly the most splendid. The ancient city on the western coast of modern-day Turkey, in an area then known as Asia Minor, was once among the wealthiest places in the region. Indeed, by the time that the magnificent temple was completed, Ephesus already had a population of 200,000 and was the centre of an important religious cult.

The first of the city's temples, constructed around 850 BC, was dedicated to Kybele, a fertility goddess and forerunner of Artemis. The centre of worship was rebuilt several times, and one of the finer temples at the site was paid for by Croesus, the immensely wealthy king of Lydia. However, in 356 BC, a madman named Herostratus burned Croesus's temple to the ground, and it was not until the late 4th century BC that the temple later included in the list of Seven Wonders was erected in its place. Reports describe how the great Temple dazzled visitors who had seen other Greek monuments, so it must have been absolutely spectacular. It was later plundered by invaders and finally destroyed when Christianity became the official religion of the Roman Empire.

THE TEMPLE TODAY
In AD 262, the Goths entered Ephesus and demolished the Temple. Later, the city was abandoned. Nothing of the Temple remained above ground until 1870, when, after seven years of excavation, British archaeologist John Turtle Wood uncovered the remains.

Terracotta clay tiles covered the roof of the Temple. There may have been an inner area left open to the skies.

The mythical griffin had the head and wings of an eagle and the body of a lion. Such statues were first brought to the Temple from central Asia as offerings to Artemis. The Greeks later designed similar statues for use as water spouts on the roof.

At the top of the columns were capitals carved in the Ionic style. They were decorated with elegant scrolls and supported the upper parts of the Temple, including the frieze.

ARTEMIS
The goddess Artemis was the daughter of Zeus and Leto and the twin sister of Apollo. For six centuries (3rd century BC to 3rd century AD) people worshipped her at the Temple. The original statue of Artemis was probably destroyed, but many copies still exist. She is similar to Kybele, the mother-goddess of Phrygia in Asia Minor, with many breasts to symbolize fertility. In Ephesus, Artemis was also the goddess of wild beasts, and she should not be confused with Artemis the goddess of hunting worshipped by the Greeks, or Diana, the Roman equivalent.

The columns were more than 18 m (60 ft) high. There were 127 in total, in rows on all four sides of the Temple. They were so densely grouped in double rows that they were said to resemble a forest.

The columns stood on drum-like marble bases, some adorned with carvings of life-sized figures painted in bright colours.

In the courtyard, merchants set out their goods. They sold small silver copies of Artemis's statue and replicas of the Temple itself.

This small statue of Artemis from Ephesus Museum is decorated with carvings of real and mythical animals. Lions, bulls, deer, panthers, and griffins on her costume emphasize Artemis's closeness to nature.

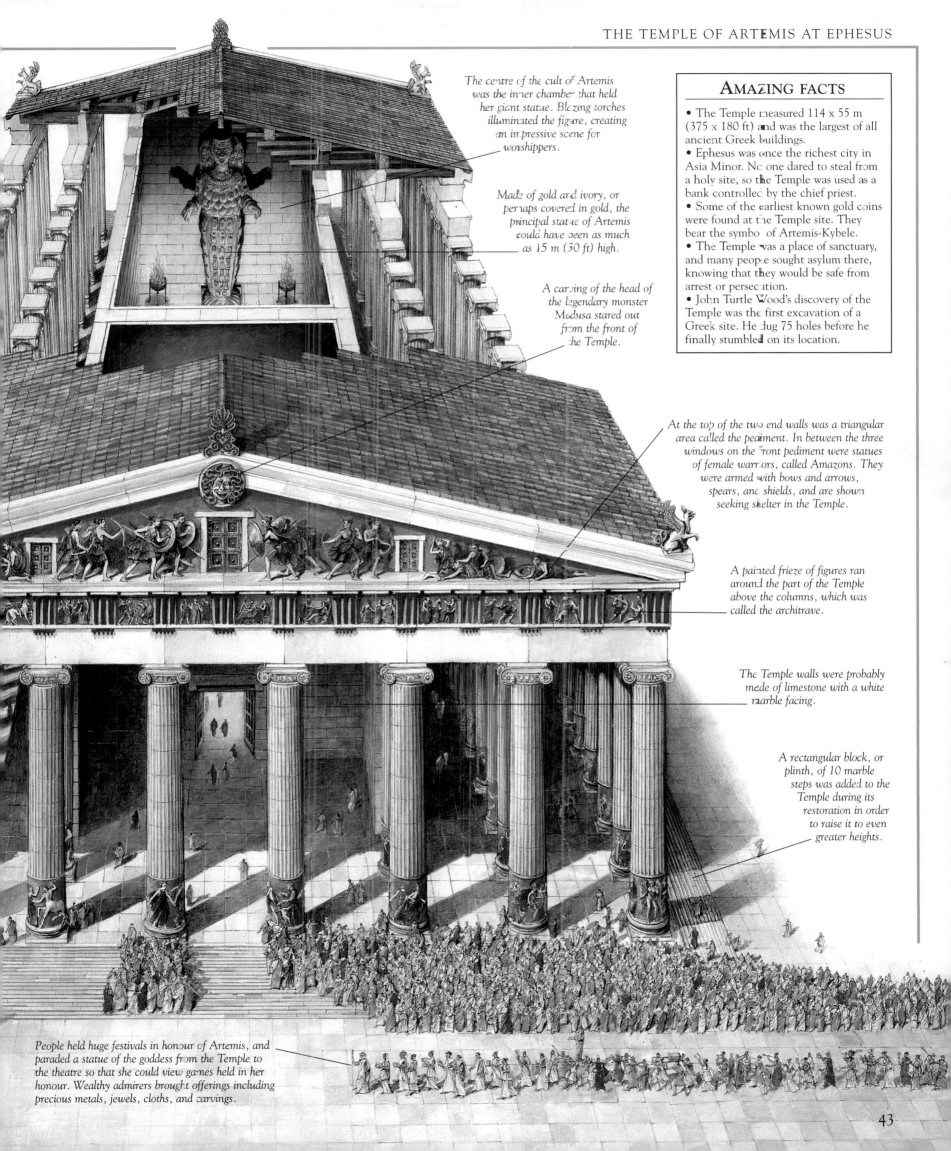

The centre of the cult of Artemis was the inner chamber that held her giant statue. Blazing torches illuminated the figure, creating an impressive scene for worshippers.

Made of gold and ivory, or perhaps covered in gold, the principal statue of Artemis could have been as much as 15 m (50 ft) high.

A carving of the head of the legendary monster Medusa stared out from the front of the Temple.

AMAZING FACTS

• The Temple measured 114 x 55 m (375 x 180 ft) and was the largest of all ancient Greek buildings.
• Ephesus was once the richest city in Asia Minor. No one dared to steal from a holy site, so the Temple was used as a bank controlled by the chief priest.
• Some of the earliest known gold coins were found at the Temple site. They bear the symbol of Artemis-Kybele.
• The Temple was a place of sanctuary, and many people sought asylum there, knowing that they would be safe from arrest or persecution.
• John Turtle Wood's discovery of the Temple was the first excavation of a Greek site. He dug 75 holes before he finally stumbled on its location.

At the top of the two end walls was a triangular area called the pediment. In between the three windows on the front pediment were statues of female warriors, called Amazons. They were armed with bows and arrows, spears, and shields, and are shown seeking shelter in the Temple.

A painted frieze of figures ran around the part of the Temple above the columns, which was called the architrave.

The Temple walls were probably made of limestone with a white marble facing.

A rectangular block, or plinth, of 10 marble steps was added to the Temple during its restoration in order to raise it to even greater heights.

People held huge festivals in honour of Artemis, and paraded a statue of the goddess from the Temple to the theatre so that she could view games held in her honour. Wealthy admirers brought offerings including precious metals, jewels, cloths, and carvings.

BUILDING THE TEMPLE

THE CONSTRUCTION OF THE MAJESTIC Temple of Artemis was an incredible achievement, considering the primitive equipment and transport available at the time. A massive labour force of architects, masons, sculptors, and teams of slaves took many years to complete the work. They carried out the project with great devotion because of its religious importance, and the results were undoubtedly breathtaking.

The sight of the finished Temple amazed ancient writers. Philo of Byzantium was clearly astonished, declaring "I have seen the walls and Hanging Gardens of ancient Babylon, the statue of Olympian Zeus, the Colossus of Rhodes, the mighty work of the high pyramids, and the tomb of Mausolus. But when I saw the Temple of Ephesus rising to the clouds, all these other wonders were put in the shade."

Columns gradually narrowed as they went up, a method that made the result more pleasing to the eye. Traditionally, Ionic columns like this one were nine times as long as they were wide.

Stonemasons carved grooves, called fluting, from the top to the bottom of the finished columns. An Ionic column usually had 24 grooves, although other styles had fewer.

As each section or drum was carved, side pegs that stuck out were left in place to act as handles for lifting. After the drums had been lowered into place, stonemasons cut the pegs away and smoothed the surface.

Ox-drawn wagons transported the drums from a quarry up to 8 km (5 miles) away. Each drum was attached to a frame and then pulled along like a giant lawn roller.

A peg in the centre of each drum interlocked with a hole in the centre of the one above. A rough surface left around the peg allowed bonding mortar to stick, gluing the sections together.

A NEW DESIGN

The foundations of the great Temple were laid on the remains of the previous temples that had occupied the site. Teams of men levelled the site, then completed the main terrace and steps before starting work on the columns. The Greek architect Cherisphron was familiar with Egyptian temple design, and the "forest of columns" that he created here was only the second Greek example of this style of architecture. Later, when faced with this majestic building, one ancient writer, Antipater of Sidon, said "Apart from Olympus, the Sun has not yet looked on anything that compares with this".

Workers built each column from as many as 12 cylindrical blocks placed one on top of the other. They used a system of levers, winches, cranes, and pulleys to lift the blocks.

Some of the finest sculptors of the age worked on the Temple. They began by drawing the subject on the stone.

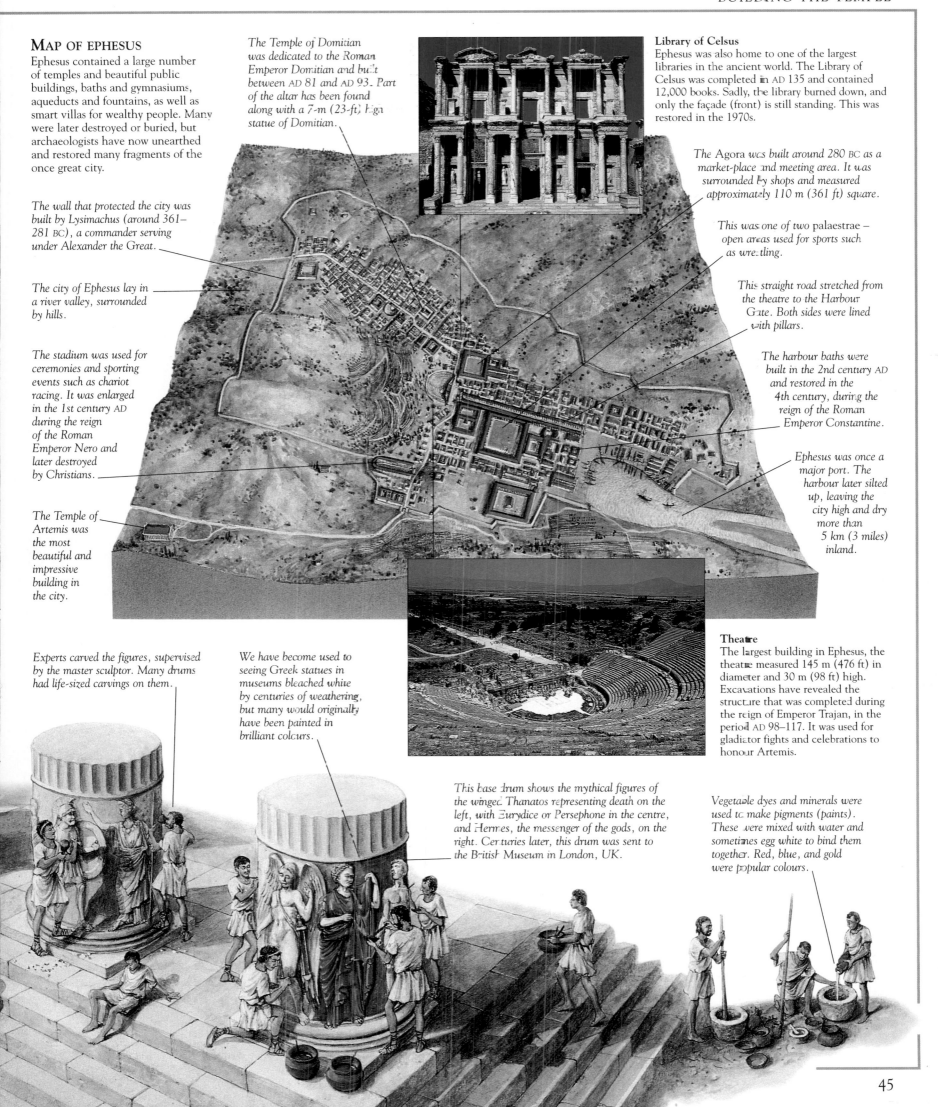

MAP OF EPHESUS

Ephesus contained a large number of temples and beautiful public buildings, baths and gymnasiums, aqueducts and fountains, as well as smart villas for wealthy people. Many were later destroyed or buried, but archaeologists have now unearthed and restored many fragments of the once great city.

The wall that protected the city was built by Lysimachus (around 361– 281 BC), a commander serving under Alexander the Great.

The city of Ephesus lay in a river valley, surrounded by hills.

The stadium was used for ceremonies and sporting events such as chariot racing. It was enlarged in the 1st century AD during the reign of the Roman Emperor Nero and later destroyed by Christians.

The Temple of Artemis was the most beautiful and impressive building in the city.

The Temple of Domitian was dedicated to the Roman Emperor Domitian and built between AD 81 and AD 93. Part of the altar has been found along with a 7-m (23-ft) high statue of Domitian.

Library of Celsus

Ephesus was also home to one of the largest libraries in the ancient world. The Library of Celsus was completed in AD 135 and contained 12,000 books. Sadly, the library burned down, and only the façade (front) is still standing. This was restored in the 1970s.

The Agora was built around 280 BC as a market-place and meeting area. It was surrounded by shops and measured approximately 110 m (361 ft) square.

This was one of two palaestrae – open areas used for sports such as wrestling.

This straight road stretched from the theatre to the Harbour Gate. Both sides were lined with pillars.

The harbour baths were built in the 2nd century AD and restored in the 4th century, during the reign of the Roman Emperor Constantine.

Ephesus was once a major port. The harbour later silted up, leaving the city high and dry more than 5 km (3 miles) inland.

Experts carved the figures, supervised by the master sculptor. Many drums had life-sized carvings on them.

We have become used to seeing Greek statues in museums bleached white by centuries of weathering, but many would originally have been painted in brilliant colours.

This base drum shows the mythical figures of the winged Thanatos representing death on the left, with Eurydice or Persephone in the centre, and Hermes, the messenger of the gods, on the right. Centuries later, this drum was sent to the British Museum in London, UK.

Theatre

The largest building in Ephesus, the theatre measured 145 m (476 ft) in diameter and 30 m (98 ft) high. Excavations have revealed the structure that was completed during the reign of Emperor Trajan, in the period AD 98–117. It was used for gladiator fights and celebrations to honour Artemis.

Vegetable dyes and minerals were used to make pigments (paints). These were mixed with water and sometimes egg white to bind them together. Red, blue, and gold were popular colours.

45

WONDERS OF WORSHIP

IN THE SAME WAY that pilgrims once flocked to the Temple of Artemis, many 21st-century worshippers are inspired to visit the centres of their faith. Christianity, Islam, Judaism, Buddhism, Hinduism, and Sikhism have all prompted their followers to create great works of architecture. Indeed, the finest of the holy buildings that are visited by pilgrims today may rival the splendour of long-vanished temples. Many of these outstanding sites have some connection with the religion's founders or leaders, or with events in the history of the faith. Often they have also become treasure houses, guarding some of the religion's most sacred or culturally valued art. In many cases they have become major shrines and centres of pilgrimage, and when all these elements exist side by side, it is not surprising that some of these buildings are among the most visited sites on Earth.

There are nine chapels around a central one, arranged in the shape of a star. Each chapel is crowned with a colourful onion-shaped dome.

The Pagoda is literally covered with gold. Pilgrims today bring even more gold leaf to stick on its walls.

ST BASIL'S CATHEDRAL

The most famous of the Russian Orthodox churches, the Cathedral of Saint Basil stands in Moscow's Red Square. It dates from the 1550s, when it was built on the orders of Tsar Ivan IV, known as "Ivan the Terrible", to give thanks for a great military victory that extended his Russian territory and also the sphere of the Orthodox Church. As heavy winter snows had collapsed the roofs of other nearby buildings, the Cathedral was designed with onion-shaped domes, which prevented the snow from settling. The Cathedral houses the remains of Saint Basil, a prophet who foretold the Great Fire of Moscow in 1547.

SHWE DAGON PAGODA

Buddhism's most important shrine is situated in Yangôn, the capital city of Burma. According to legend, two brothers brought eight sacred hairs from the Buddha's head to the site, and the temple was built there by King Oklalapak. The Pagoda is made of bricks and covered with gold and precious stones donated by the King's successors. It stands on a hill above the city, rising to a height of 99 m (326 ft). The temple complex is surrounded by smaller pagodas and temples with many bells and statues of sacred animals.

THE GREAT MOSQUE AT MECCA

Mecca in Saudi Arabia is the holiest city in the Islamic world, and Muslim people turn towards it in prayer five times a day. It is also the duty of all Muslims to make the pilgrimage (*hajj*) to Mecca at least once in their lifetime. The city was the birthplace around AD 570 of Muhammad the Prophet, whose flight from Mecca marked the start of Islam. At the centre of the Great Mosque stands a cube-shaped shrine called the *Kaaba*, which contains the Black Stone. It is said that this stone was given to Adam, the first man, and that the *Kaaba* was built at the command of God.

Pilgrims at the Great Mosque circle the shrine in the centre of the courtyard.

A 60-m (196-ft) marble causeway connects the walkway around the lake to the Temple.

THE WAILING WALL

The Western Wall (known to non-Jewish people as the Wailing Wall) stands in Jerusalem, Israel. It is the only surviving part of the temple at the centre of the Jewish faith. The first temple to be built on the site was constructed by King Solomon, and the wall that remains was part of a later temple built by King Herod, which was destroyed by the Romans in AD 70. The name "Wailing" refers to the sadness of Jews at this act. Male and female visitors worship separately, and some place written prayers in crevices in the Wall.

MEENAKSHI TEMPLE

One of many beautiful temple complexes in southern India, the Meenakshi Temple at Madurai attracts thousands of Hindu worshippers. The site is dedicated to Meenakshi, who was the princess of Madurai and the companion of the Hindu god Shiva. The temple complex includes 12 tall gate towers, which are carved with many figures. Within the tallest temple is the Hall of a Thousand Pillars, which is decorated with brightly coloured images of gods and goddesses. There is also an ancient pool, where pilgrims bathe in holy water.

ST PETER'S BASILICA

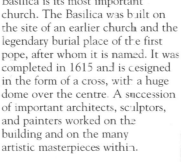

The Vatican is a tiny independent state in the city of Rome. It is the headquarters of the Roman Catholic faith, and St Peter's Basilica is its most important church. The Basilica was built on the site of an earlier church and the legendary burial place of the first pope, after whom it is named. It was completed in 1615 and is designed in the form of a cross, with a huge dome over the centre. A succession of important architects, sculptors, and painters worked on the building and on the many artistic masterpieces within.

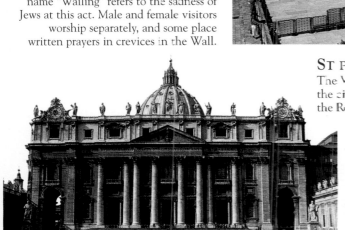

THE GOLDEN TEMPLE

This spectacular building in Amritsar, India, is the most important pilgrimage site for Sikhs. The temple is the second shrine to occupy the site in the holy city, which was once the home of Guru Nanak, the founder of the Sikh religion. The first temple, which was completed in 1601, was built on an island in an artificially made pool. It was later destroyed, and the construction of a new temple began in 1764. Workers used marble and copper and added 400 kg (882 lb) of gold leaf to the upper part of the temple, which gives the building its name.

Images of flowers and religious hymns decorate the Temple.

Entrances on all sides of the Temple symbolize its openness to everyone.

The Temple contains the Guru Granth Sahib, *the holy book of the Sikhs.*

A gateway marks the entrance to the Temple complex. A treasury above it houses golden doors and jewelled canopies.

MORE ANCIENT WONDERS

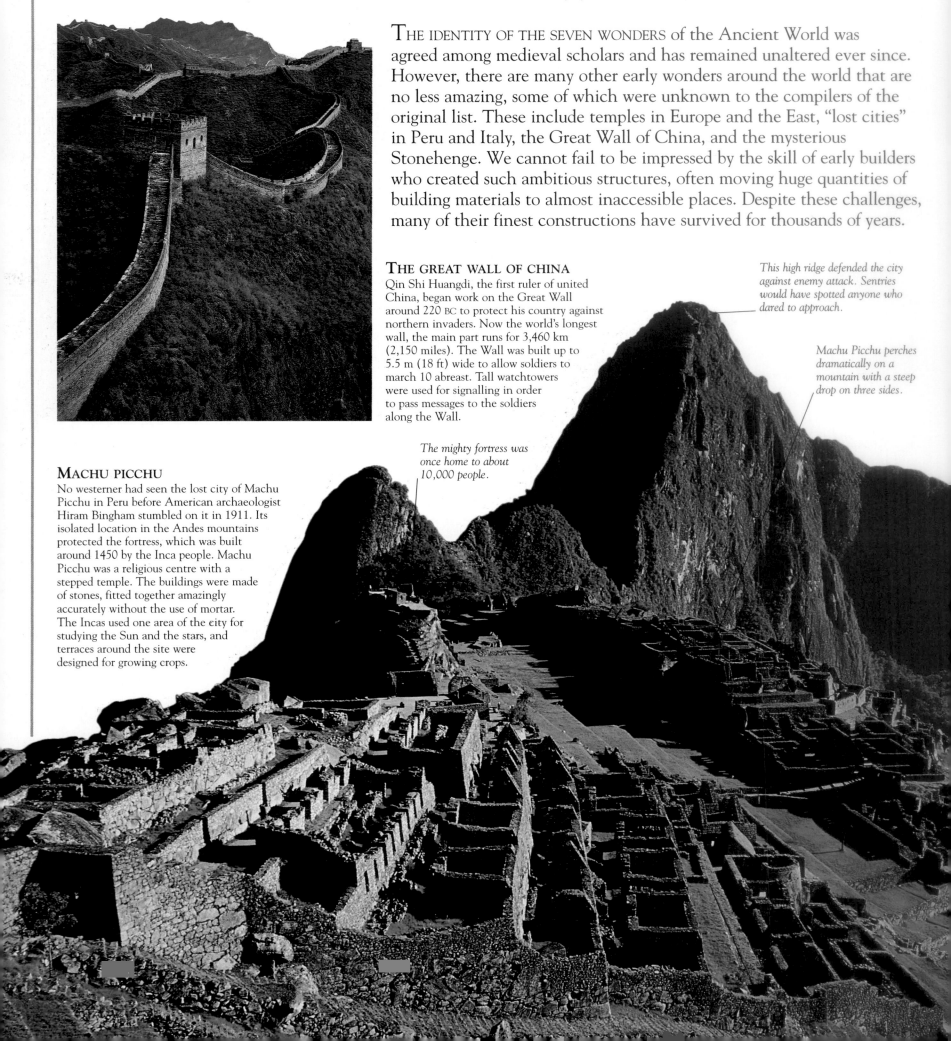

THE IDENTITY OF THE SEVEN WONDERS of the Ancient World was agreed among medieval scholars and has remained unaltered ever since. However, there are many other early wonders around the world that are no less amazing, some of which were unknown to the compilers of the original list. These include temples in Europe and the East, "lost cities" in Peru and Italy, the Great Wall of China, and the mysterious Stonehenge. We cannot fail to be impressed by the skill of early builders who created such ambitious structures, often moving huge quantities of building materials to almost inaccessible places. Despite these challenges, many of their finest constructions have survived for thousands of years.

THE GREAT WALL OF CHINA

Qin Shi Huangdi, the first ruler of united China, began work on the Great Wall around 220 BC to protect his country against northern invaders. Now the world's longest wall, the main part runs for 3,460 km (2,150 miles). The Wall was built up to 5.5 m (18 ft) wide to allow soldiers to march 10 abreast. Tall watchtowers were used for signalling in order to pass messages to the soldiers along the Wall.

This high ridge defended the city against enemy attack. Sentries would have spotted anyone who dared to approach.

Machu Picchu perches dramatically on a mountain with a steep drop on three sides.

The mighty fortress was once home to about 10,000 people.

MACHU PICCHU

No westerner had seen the lost city of Machu Picchu in Peru before American archaeologist Hiram Bingham stumbled on it in 1911. Its isolated location in the Andes mountains protected the fortress, which was built around 1450 by the Inca people. Machu Picchu was a religious centre with a stepped temple. The buildings were made of stones, fitted together amazingly accurately without the use of mortar. The Incas used one area of the city for studying the Sun and the stars, and terraces around the site were designed for growing crops.

BOROBUDUR

The world's largest Buddhist temple, Borobudur, on the Indonesian island of Java was built between AD 778 and 850. Built from volcanic stone, it is a pyramid-like structure reaching 31.5 m (103 ft) at its highest point. The temple consists of a series of platforms, which represent stages in the life of a Buddhist on the way from ignorance to nirvana (heavenly bliss). It includes over 500 figures of Buddha as well as bell-shaped shrines, each containing a statue.

POMPEII

In AD 79, the Italian city of Pompeii was devastated by the eruption of the nearby volcano, Mount Vesuvius. As many as 2,000 inhabitants fell victim to poisonous gases or were killed under a rain of ash that buried the city to a depth of 4 m (13 ft). However, the ash also preserved the buildings, which were excavated many centuries later. Archaeologists uncovered a city frozen in time: a theatre, villas, temples, and shops. Many buildings contained wall-paintings and personal objects that have provided information about the daily lives of ancient people.

Canals and reservoirs once supplied the Khmer people with water during the dry season.

ANGKOR WAT

Once the capital of the Khmer Empire, Angkor Wat in Cambodia is part of a vast temple complex built in the 12th century by King Suryavarman II, who was buried there. The city was attacked in 1431 and then abandoned. A few monks remained there, but it was unknown to the West until 1861, when French naturalist Henri Mouhot discovered it. Archaeologists later found a temple dedicated to the Hindu god Vishnu with many beautiful carvings and huge moats and reservoirs. Sadly, the buildings were damaged during wars in the 20th century.

THE ACROPOLIS

The Acropolis in Athens, Greece, stands 45 m (148 ft) high. Its name means "city at the top", and it was an area of high ground that could be defended against attackers. Once the home of the city's kings, for many years the Acropolis was the religious centre of Athens. The most famous temple on the Acropolis is the Parthenon. It dates from 447 to 432 BC and was built by the sculptor Phidias, who created the statue of Zeus at Olympia.

Upright blocks topped by horizontal slabs formed a ring around the stones in the middle, which were grouped in threes.

STONEHENGE

These standing stones in south-west England date from around 3000 BC. Stonehenge began with a circular ditch to which earth, stone, and wooden structures were added over almost 2,000 years. Many experts believe that people managed to drag the giant stones to the site – a great feat as some blocks weighed up to 50 tonnes. Stonehenge may have an astronomical function, but precisely who built it and why remain unknown.

This circle of standing stones and the inner horseshoe shape were built around 1900 BC.

WONDERFUL PALACES AND CASTLES

RULERS HAVE TRADITIONALLY emphasized their wealth and power by building majestic palaces, but in troubled times they have also needed to defend their residences against attack, leading to the creation of mighty castles like the Tower of London and the Krak des Chevaliers. After the invention of gunpowder, castle walls had to be strengthened against cannon fire, and vantage points for snipers with muskets were introduced to defend many strongholds against attack. Some structures, such as the Alhambra, combined the features of both fortress and palace, while others, like King Ludwig II's Neuschwanstein, the Imperial Palace, and Louis XIV's Versailles are monuments to the lavish lifestyles of their creators.

KRAK DES CHEVALIERS

This massive fortress was described by T. E. Lawrence (Lawrence of Arabia) as "the best-preserved and most admirable castle in the world". The Krak des Chevaliers at Qal'at al-Hisn in Syria was built during the 12th and 13th centuries on a hilltop on the site of an earlier Muslim fortress. It was guarded by 2,000 men and occupied by crusader knights, who were trying to win control of the Holy Land. The castle was finally overpowered in 1271, and the knights moved their headquarters to Rhodes.

The castle has two thick ring-shaped walls and a moat, which helped it to withstand long sieges.

Now one of Germany's most visited tourist attractions, the design of Neuschwanstein inspired Walt Disney World's "Magic Kingdom" castle.

NEUSCHWANSTEIN

King Ludwig II ascended the throne of Bavaria in 1861 at the age of 18. Soon afterwards, he began to build this extraordinary hilltop castle in the Bavarian Alps. Inspired by mythology and the operas of Richard Wagner, which were based on German legends, Ludwig designed his home to resemble a fairy-tale castle, complete with towers, spires, and even an artificial cave, and he decorated it inside in a variety of bizarre styles. Ludwig had little time to enjoy his fantasy home – barely 100 days after he moved in, he was declared unfit to rule and moved to another of his properties, where he later died.

Although Ludwig's castle looks medieval and solid enough to withstand invaders, it was built as recently as the 19th century.

Work on the White Tower was completed in 1097.

The battlements of the White Tower are 27 m (90 ft) high.

THE TOWER OF LONDON

Now a popular tourist attraction, the Tower of London has long been at the centre of British history. Over many centuries it has been used as a fortress, a prison, and as a strongroom for the Crown Jewels. Built beside the River Thames on the instructions of William the Conqueror, the Tower later became a royal residence and housed the Royal Mint, where coins were made. The White Tower was the first part to be built. Thick walls and a moat were added later, along with many other towers, including the Lion Tower, which contained the royal menagerie, or zoo. For many centuries traitors were imprisoned and executed at the Tower.

THE IMPERIAL PALACE

A city within a city, the Forbidden City and Imperial Palace lie at the centre of Beijing (Peking) in China. Its construction began under Emperor Zhu Di, who moved his capital there from Nanking in 1421, and it remained the home of China's rulers until 1911, when their empire finally collapsed. The Forbidden City, which got its name because common people and foreigners could not enter it, takes the form of a large square surrounded by a moat and a high wall. Inside there are courtyards and gardens and a palace complex with 9,000 rooms. This was once occupied by the emperor and his family as well as courtiers, soldiers, and servants. Today the Forbidden City is preserved as a museum of China's past and is open to all visitors.

THE ALHAMBRA

Granada in southern Spain was once ruled by Moors from the north of Africa. They built a beautiful palace, called the Alhambra. Its name means "the red", in Arabic, after the colour of its bricks. Work on the Alhambra was started in the 13th century by Muhammad I al Ghalib. At its heart is a fortress with 23 towers, but this is only part of a complex that includes a beautiful royal palace with spectacular rooms, courtyards, gardens, and fountains. Its walls are decorated with colourful ceramic tiles and carved stonework. Some of its structure was destroyed after Christian rulers seized control of the region, but enough remains to make the Alhambra one of the world's greatest examples of Islamic architecture.

Himeji Castle is also known as "White Heron Castle" because its walls and roofs resemble a heron ready to take off.

The carved stonework of the Court of the Lions features many detailed designs.

VERSAILLES PALACE

The Palace of Versailles near Paris, France, was originally the hunting lodge of King Louis XIII, but in 1660 his son, Louis XIV, began an ambitious expansion programme. His plans included not only the architecture of the building but also the landscaping of its extensive gardens, with many fountains and statues. Work on the Palace took almost 100 years to complete. Its most celebrated feature was the fabulous Hall of Mirrors, which was used for grand ceremonies. The Palace was large enough to house as many as 1,000 courtiers and 4,000 servants. It was the setting for extravagant entertainments until the royal family was overthrown during the French Revolution of 1789.

HIMEJI CASTLE

The town of Himeji, to the west of Osaka, Japan, grew up around Himeji Castle, an elegant fortress with a superb defence system. It is thought to have been started in 1346 by a feudal lord named Sadanori Akamatsu. In 1601, it was partly rebuilt by Ikeda Terumasa, a military ruler who, with the help of thousands of workers, took nine years to complete the present structure. The castle includes such features as holes for firing arrows and guns at the enemy and moats and high walls with sharp edges to deter invaders. The castle was so well designed that it was never besieged or damaged by warfare, so it has survived as Japan's finest medieval fortress.

Göreme is a National Park and attracts as many as 600,000 visitors a year.

CAPPADOCIA ROCK DWELLINGS

Amongst Earth's strangest landscapes, Cappadocia includes cave-like dwellings that people have carved out of rock to create an underground city. This spectacular area of geological formations is situated at Göreme in Anatolia, Turkey. Around three million years ago, nearby volcanoes spewed out lava, which hardened into rock. Since then the softer rocks have been eroded by wind and water, leaving the harder ones standing out as rock pinnacles and cones known as "fairy chimneys", some of them 40 m (130 ft) high.

DJENNÉ MOSQUE

The Friday Mosque at Djenné in Mali, West Africa, is the world's largest mud building. Created in 1906–07, the whole structure is built out of sun-dried mud. The Mosque resembles a giant sandcastle with turrets and spires capped by ostrich eggs, regarded as symbols of fertility and purity. As the rivers rise during the rainy season, Djenné becomes an island and part of the structure is washed away. Each year in the following dry season the Mosque's walls have to be replastered to prevent it from falling down.

WEIRD WONDERS

THE WORLD IS FULL of marvellous structures made by people. Some are considered wonders because they are great feats of engineering or examples of beautiful design, but the wonders here are special because they are all strange and unique. They include a pagoda dangerously balanced on a golden rock and an equally precarious leaning tower, while other bizarre buildings, such as a huge mosque built entirely of mud and a fantastic cathedral adorned with plant-like shapes, demonstrate a wealth of human creativity. Perhaps even more remarkable are a city carved out of volcanic rocks, huge pictures that can be seen only from the air, and the world's most gigantic steel arch. Each in it own way defies our sense of order and logic, and yet each is undeniably wonderful.

The Tower reaches a height of 55 m (179 ft).

By the end of the 20th century, the Tower was leaning by an alarming 5.5°, and the top overhung the base by 5.2 m (17 ft).

NAZCA LINES

Dating from the 1st century AD, the Nazca Lines on Peru's south coast were cut into the earth by removing rocks and topsoil. They include geometric shapes as well as plants and animals; the spider shown above is 50 m (164 ft) across, while other images are even larger. The lines are remarkable because they are properly visible only from the air, leading some people to suppose that they were carved by extra-terrestrials. In spite of much recent speculation, their origin remains a mystery.

SAGRADA FAMILIA

Work on this extraordinary cathedral, the Sagrada Familia (Holy Family) in Barcelona, Spain, began in 1884, but it is still unfinished. Designed by Spanish architect Antonio Gaudí, it features three façades, each with gigantic towers. Unlike any other Roman Catholic church, its stone resembles a growing, living thing, decorated with colourful ornamentation.

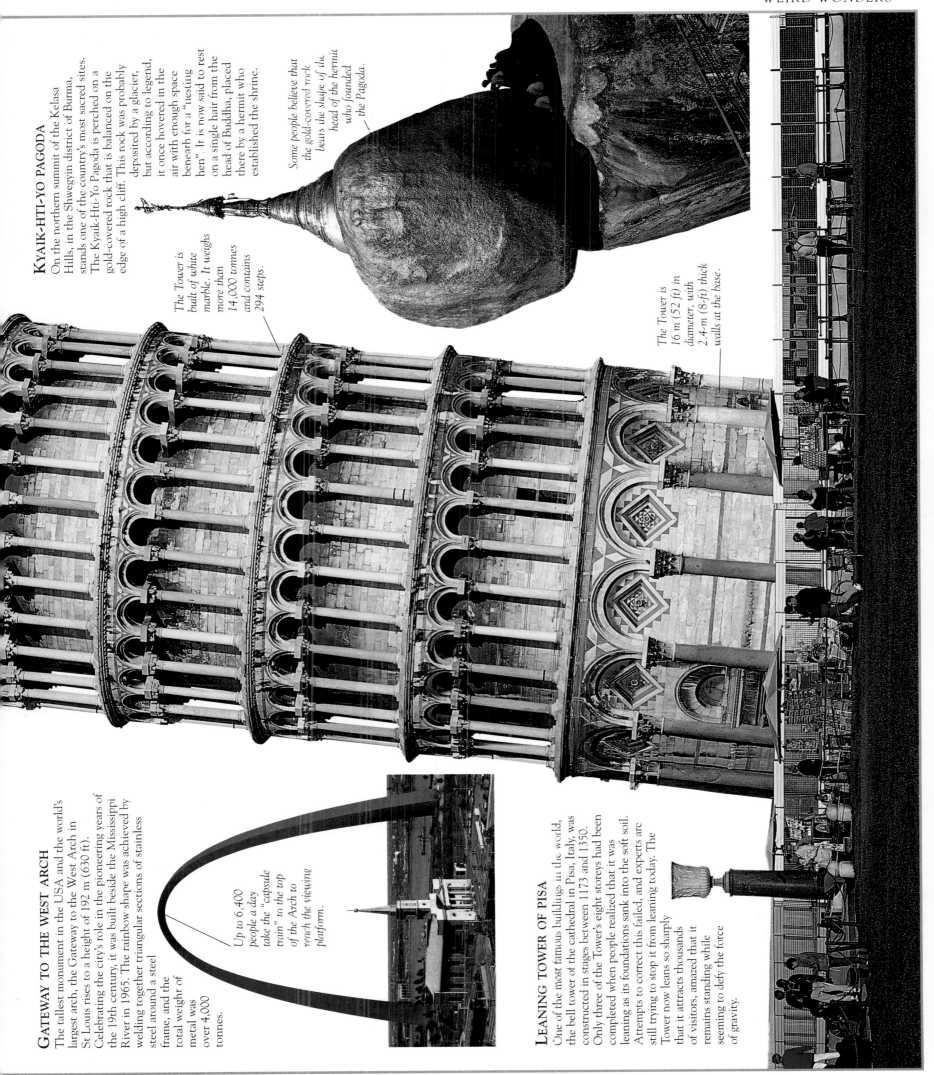

KYAIK-HTI-YO PAGODA

On the northern summit of the Kelasa Hills, in the Shwegyin district of Burma, stands one of the country's most sacred sites. The Kyaik-Hti-Yo Pagoda is perched on a gold-covered rock that is balanced on the edge of a high cliff. This rock was probably deposited by a glacier, but according to legend, it once hovered in the air with enough space beneath for a "nesting hen." It is now said to rest on a single hair from the head of Buddha, placed there by a hermit who established the shrine.

Some people believe that the gold-covered rock bears the shape of the head of the hermit who founded the Pagoda.

The Tower is built of white marble. It weighs more than 14,000 tonnes and contains 294 steps.

The Tower is 16 m (52 ft) in diameter, with 2.4-m (8-ft) thick walls at the base.

GATEWAY TO THE WEST ARCH

The tallest monument in the USA and the world's largest arch, the Gateway to the West Arch in St Louis rises to a height of 192 m (630 ft). Celebrating the city's role in the pioneering years of the 19th century, it was built beside the Mississippi River in 1965. The rainbow shape was achieved by welding together triangular sections of stainless steel around a steel frame, and the total weight of metal was over 4,000 tonnes.

Up to 6,400 people a day take the "capsule train" to the top of the Arch to reach the viewing platform.

LEANING TOWER OF PISA

One of the most famous buildings in the world, the bell tower of the cathedral in Pisa, Italy, was constructed in stages between 1173 and 1350. Only three of the Tower's eight storeys had been completed when people realized that it was leaning as its foundations sank into the soft soil. Attempts to correct this failed, and experts are still trying to stop it from leaning today. The Tower now leans so sharply that it attracts thousands of visitors, amazed that it remains standing while seeming to defy the force of gravity.

WONDERS OF ENGINEERING

A mighty boring machine created tunnels large enough to carry passenger and freight trains.

HUMAN ACHIEVEMENTS IN ENGINEERING and art enabled the construction of the Seven Wonders of the Ancient World, and as later technological advances took place, people began to build more and more exciting structures. These pages reveal some of the awe-inspiring results of their efforts: a giant aqueduct (a bridge for transporting water), a great canal, a mighty dam, a spectacular bridge, an underwater tunnel, major sea defences, and a unique airport. Without advanced technical skills, none of these structures could have been built. However, through a combination of inspiration and perseverance, their creators overcame the most challenging obstacles to produce structures that previous generations could only dream of. We may well wonder what new marvels may be possible as engineers advance into the 21st century.

THE CHANNEL TUNNEL

Work on a tunnel under the sea linking Great Britain and France began in 1987, and it opened in 1994. Enormous quantities of earth were removed to create a total of 151.5 km (94 miles) of tunnels. The Channel Tunnel has two main tunnels, each 50 km (31 miles) long and 7.6 m (25 ft) in diameter, bored at an average depth of 45 m (148 ft) beneath the seabed. Transport is by passenger trains travelling at speeds of up to 160 km/h (100 mph) or by shuttle trains carrying vehicles and passengers.

The towers of the Golden Gate Bridge soar to a height of 227 m (746 ft).

THE GOLDEN GATE BRIDGE

For many years the world's longest and tallest bridge, the Golden Gate Bridge was one of the 20th century's greatest feats of engineering. Its designer, Joseph Strauss, spent years planning how to complete the structure, overcoming such problems as the threat of earthquakes and the need to sink the south pier 30 m (98 ft) into the seabed in fast-flowing water. Disaster almost struck during construction when a ship collided with the bridge, but the famous landmark eventually opened to traffic in 1937.

THE PANAMA CANAL

Before the Panama Canal was built, to get from the Atlantic to the Pacific Ocean, ships were forced to sail right around South America. Today, however, the 82-km (50-mile) Canal connects the Atlantic and Pacific Oceans, cutting east-west distances by as much as 12,875 km (8,000 miles). Progress on this massive project was far from easy and thousands of people died during construction. After the failure of an earlier attempt, work on the canal resumed in 1904. Over the next 10 years 75,000 workers dynamited and dug out more than 180 million tonnes of rock and earth to create this modern wonder.

DELTAWERKEN

In 1986, the creation of an immense sea barrier on the south-western coast of the Netherlands finally put an end to the terrible floods that had killed thousands of people and devastated valuable farm land. The Delta Project, or *Deltawerken*, consisted of a series of huge dams that stretched for a total of 30 km (18 miles). The most ambitious piece of engineering is the 2.8-km (1.75-mile) movable barrier across the Oosterschelde estuary, which consists of 65 concrete piers, each the height of a 12-storey building and weighing 16,330 tonnes, with 31 steel gates that are lowered during high tides to prevent flood damage.

THE PONT DU GARD

The ancient Romans were expert engineers, and evidence of their many technical achievements survives to this day. By the first century AD, they had built this aqueduct near the city of Nîmes in southern France. It was used to deliver great volumes of water to the city from a spring at Uzès, 50 km (31 miles) away. The aqueduct crosses the Gard River (its name means "Bridge of the Gard"), and it is 275 m (900 ft) long. It consists of three tiers of arches, rising to a total height of 49 m (160 ft) and is made of limestone blocks fixed together without mortar.

The building of the Dam led to the creation of Lake Mead, which is one of the largest artificially formed lakes in the world.

THE HOOVER DAM

In the hottest, driest part of the United States, the Hoover Dam brings vital supplies of water to millions of people. By harnessing the power of nature, engineers have made water available not only for the irrigation of farm land in Nevada and Arizona but also for the production of hydro-electric power. Work on the Dam began on the Colorado River in 1931 and took five years to complete. The structure is 379 m (1,244 ft) long and stands 221 m (726 ft) high. For 22 years it was the world's highest dam, and it contains enough concrete to build a 5-m (16-ft) wide road all the way from San Francisco to New York City.

Roads leading to the Hoover Dam seem tiny by comparison, and trucks look like ants next to the mighty structure.

Kansai is the first ever ocean airport. With no neighbours to disturb, it can operate for 24 hours a day.

KANSAI INTERNATIONAL AIRPORT

The world's largest artificially made island is home to Japan's extraordinary Kansai airport. Measuring 4 x 1.2 km (2.5 x 0.75 miles), the island stands 5 km (3 miles) off the coast, connected by a single bridge. Before work could begin on the airport, divers used 48,000 concrete blocks to build a gigantic sea barrier against storm damage. Next, a million columns and 69 enormous steel chambers were driven into the seabed, and three mountains were flattened so that their earth could be poured into the sea. Built on soft clay, the whole island is slowly sinking, but the airport terminal is steadily raised by powerful hydraulic jacks.

WONDERS OF TRANSPORT

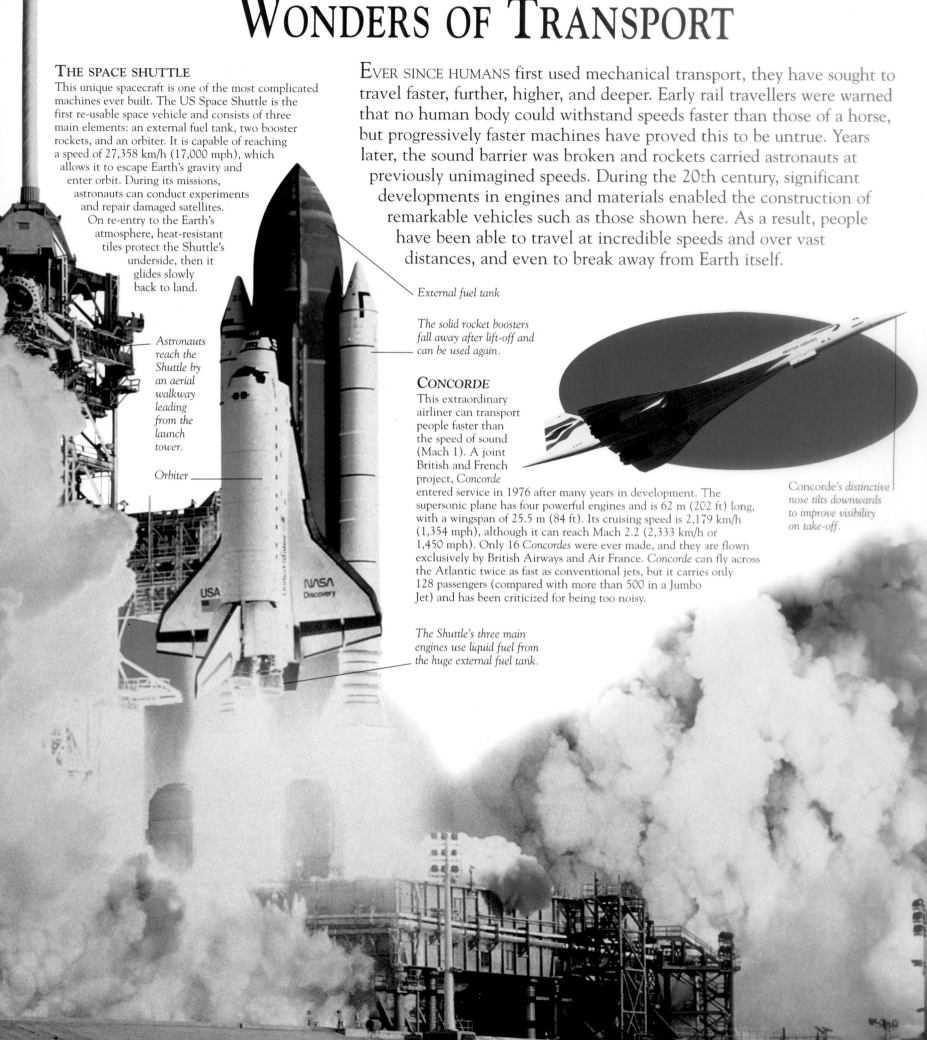

THE SPACE SHUTTLE

This unique spacecraft is one of the most complicated machines ever built. The US Space Shuttle is the first re-usable space vehicle and consists of three main elements: an external fuel tank, two booster rockets, and an orbiter. It is capable of reaching a speed of 27,358 km/h (17,000 mph), which allows it to escape Earth's gravity and enter orbit. During its missions, astronauts can conduct experiments and repair damaged satellites. On re-entry to the Earth's atmosphere, heat-resistant tiles protect the Shuttle's underside, then it glides slowly back to land.

Astronauts reach the Shuttle by an aerial walkway leading from the launch tower.

Orbiter

EVER SINCE HUMANS first used mechanical transport, they have sought to travel faster, further, higher, and deeper. Early rail travellers were warned that no human body could withstand speeds faster than those of a horse, but progressively faster machines have proved this to be untrue. Years later, the sound barrier was broken and rockets carried astronauts at previously unimagined speeds. During the 20th century, significant developments in engines and materials enabled the construction of remarkable vehicles such as those shown here. As a result, people have been able to travel at incredible speeds and over vast distances, and even to break away from Earth itself.

External fuel tank

The solid rocket boosters fall away after lift-off and can be used again.

CONCORDE

This extraordinary airliner can transport people faster than the speed of sound (Mach 1). A joint British and French project, *Concorde* entered service in 1976 after many years in development. The supersonic plane has four powerful engines and is 62 m (202 ft) long, with a wingspan of 25.5 m (84 ft). Its cruising speed is 2,179 km/h (1,354 mph), although it can reach Mach 2.2 (2,333 km/h or 1,450 mph). Only 16 *Concordes* were ever made, and they are flown exclusively by British Airways and Air France. *Concorde* can fly across the Atlantic twice as fast as conventional jets, but it carries only 128 passengers (compared with more than 500 in a Jumbo Jet) and has been criticized for being too noisy.

Concorde's distinctive nose tilts downwards to improve visibility on take-off.

The Shuttle's three main engines use liquid fuel from the huge external fuel tank.

Thrust SSC hurtles across the desert to break the sound barrier.

The colossal Breitling Orbiter 3 balloon is 55 m (180 ft) tall.

THRUST SSC

For almost 100 years, drivers steadily raised the land speed record from the 63.16 km/h (39.25 mph) set in 1898, but breaking the sound barrier was the ultimate challenge. This was finally achieved on 15 October 1997 at Black Rock Desert, Nevada, USA, when the *Thrust SSC*, driven by the British pilot Andy Green, averaged a phenomenal speed of 1,227.99 km/h (763.04 mph). An enormous vehicle, 16.5 m (54 ft) long and powered by two 110,000-horsepower Rolls-Royce jet engines, *Thrust SSC* actually reached an even higher speed, but the land speed record rules require the figure to be an average over two separate runs.

BREITLING ORBITER BALLOON

After almost 20 years and many failed attempts by others, the first non-stop round-the-world balloon flight was achieved in 1999. The pilots, Bertrand Piccard from Switzerland and Brian Jones from the UK, travelled in a high-tech cabin with life-support and communications equipment. *Breitling Orbiter 3* took off from Switzerland and crossed the globe from west to east, covering a complete circle of 42,810 km (26,600 miles) in 19 days, 1 hour and 49 minutes. It then extended the record distance even further by landing in southern Egypt.

THE TELEFÉRICO MÉRIDA

Cable cars are often the only practical way of transporting people and goods to locations at the top of high mountains. The Teleférico Mérida, which links Mérida City in the Venezuelan Andes with Pico Espejo (Mirror Peak), is the world's longest and highest cable car system. It starts at an elevation of 1,639.5 m (5,379 ft) above sea level and rises in four stages to 4,763 m (15,629 ft). It runs for 12.8 km (8 miles), crossing forests, canyons, and rivers in the Sierra Nevada National Park. Each of its eight cars holds up to 45 people, and the whole journey takes almost an hour.

THE BULLET TRAIN

Known to westerners as the Bullet Train, the Japanese *Shinkansen* (new high-speed railways) entered service in the 1960s. Since that time, the trains have carried as many as 3 billion passengers. These streamlined electric trains operate on specially built straight tracks that allow them to travel at very high speeds. The Series 500 trains on the Kokura-Hiroshima line achieved the world record for a scheduled service, with an average speed of 261.8 km/h (163 mph). They also have a near-perfect safety record, making them admired as models for high-speed trains throughout the world.

NAUTILE SUBMERSIBLE

The French-built *Nautile* is a small submersible vehicle that can carry three people to a depth of 6,000 m (19,685 ft), making it possible to explore all but the very deepest oceans. Costing £12 million to build, it weighs 19.3 tonnes and is 8 m (26 ft 3 in) long and 2.7 m (8 ft 11 in) wide. It is made of a strong titanium metal alloy, with walls 10 cm (4 in) thick to withstand the great pressure of water above it. *Nautile* is electrically powered and has thrusters that make it easy to manoeuvre, while sonar devices help it to retrieve objects from the seabed. It also carries cameras and advanced communications equipment and can send out a tethered robot to explore deep inside the wrecks of ships such as the *Titanic*.

WONDERFUL INVENTIONS

AN INVENTION IS SOMETHING THAT WAS CREATED as a result of human effort and that did not exist before. The ideas behind many inventions are so original and important that they have changed the course of history. Breakthroughs that have enabled other crucial developments to take place are particularly significant. Societies that had the wheel, such as the Romans with their chariots, progressed further than those that did not. Electricity brought light and power to our houses and allowed new industries to develop. Vaccination has saved the lives of countless millions of people, while cloning marks only the beginning of a revolution in genetic engineering. Printing presses have enabled the wide transmission of knowledge, and now satellites orbiting in space make instant global communication possible, while industrial robots involved in mass production have taken over some of the more monotonous and dangerous jobs in many factories.

Simple wooden wheel

Wheel from an E-type Jaguar car (1960s)

THE WHEEL

No one knows who invented the wheel, but it is difficult to imagine how people ever managed without it. The development of entire societies, such as those in the Americas, was limited by their lack of wheels. As a result, they had to rely on animals for transport over land and had no way of moving very heavy loads. If the wheel had never been invented, today there would be no cars, trains, bicycles, or even roller-skates or skateboards. The first wheels, made of wood, date from around 3500 BC. Improved spoked wheels were used for chariots and carriages and even for sports cars in more recent times.

Streamlined bicycles with special wheels have steadily raised the world record speed.

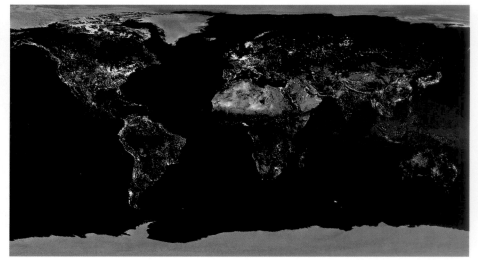

ELECTRICITY

Lit up at night, the cities of the world are clearly seen from space, as shown in this satellite image. The use of electricity that made this possible dates back little more than 100 years – the first homes received an electric supply in the 1880s. Electricity is the only source of energy that can be transmitted from one place to another by cables. Now our houses depend on it for a host of equipment, including refrigerators, washing machines, and televisions, while in the wider world industrial machinery and transport, such as railways, rely on electricity for their power.

CLONING

A clone is an individual organism grown from just one cell belonging to its parent and that is identical to the parent. The first large mammal to be cloned was Dolly the sheep at the Roslin Institute in Edinburgh, Scotland, in 1996. DNA (the material from which all living things are made) was taken from an adult sheep, and an embryo was formed and implanted in another sheep. This development, called genetic engineering, is significant because scientists can now select certain desirable genes and eliminate faulty ones, a process that may one day be applied to human beings.

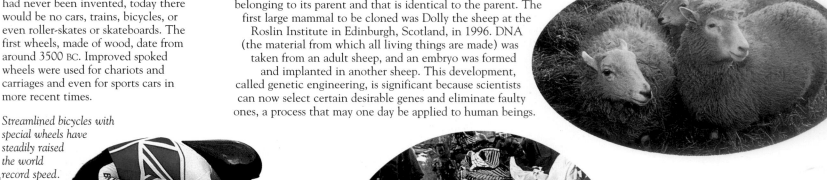

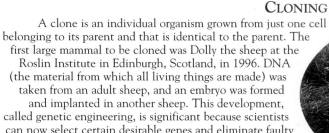

VACCINATIONS

A vaccine is a tiny dose of the infecting agent of a disease, which has been specially treated to make it safe. The vaccination provides immunity, or protection, against the disease. In 1796, the British doctor Edward Jenner deliberately infected a boy by injecting him with cowpox, making him immune to smallpox – a deadly disease that has since been completely eradicated. Throughout the world, vaccination has become a major lifesaver as vaccines have been developed to protect people against other diseases that had previously killed millions, including diphtheria, tetanus, tuberculosis, polio, and measles.

ROBOTS

For a long time, robots (from the Czech word *robota*, meaning "work") were just the dream of inventors. They became a reality in the second half of the 20th century when all the necessary technology, such as electronics and computers, was sufficiently developed to produce a "mechanical human". However, most robots do not resemble people but have arm-like manipulators designed to grip a tool and perform a special function, such as welding parts on a car. Robots follow a computer programme that "teaches" them to perform a task and repeat it non-stop, which human operators would find exhausting. Today there are more than 700,000 industrial robots in use around the world.

THE PRINTING PRESS

If printing had not been invented, you would not be reading this book. Before the late 15th century, all books were hand written and few people outside the Church had access to them. The invention of printing with movable type, where each letter is added to the printing press by hand, began a process that made books available to everyone and helped in the wider transmission of knowledge. Modern methods have made cheap colour printing practical and, by using huge rolls of paper, more than 100,000 newspapers per hour can be printed on rotary presses like the one shown here.

COMMUNICATIONS SATELLITES

A satellite is anything that orbits a planet. The idea of communication by satellite was suggested in 1945, and the first human-made satellite, called *Sputnik I*, was launched by the Soviets in 1957. Launched by rocket or Space Shuttle, there are now thousands of satellites in orbit, creating a network that permits international telephone calls, television, radio, Internet connections, and accurate global positioning for ships and aircraft. Signals are transmitted from Earth, then sent from orbiting satellites to other satellites or locations on the ground, which overcomes the need for cable connections.

Satellites are expensive to build, but they have totally revolutionized world communications.

Most satellites orbit at a speed that allows them to remain above the same part of the Earth all the time.

Powered by solar cells that keep their batteries charged, satellites can remain in orbit for many years.

NATURAL WONDERS

HOWEVER AMAZING, the human-made wonders in this book are easily surpassed by some of the wonders created by the forces of nature. Natural phenomena that have occurred since the Earth was formed are often on a scale that no human activity can match. The immense power of flowing water has produced great cave systems, carved huge canyons, and shaped mighty waterfalls. The plates that make up the Earth's surface have collided and volcanoes have erupted to raise huge mountains. Life-forms from coral reefs to tropical trees cover vast areas of the planet, and even the atmosphere is capable of producing magical effects that have astonished people for millennia. It is not surprising that many natural wonders are also among the world's most popular tourist attractions.

MOUNT EVEREST
The world's highest mountain, Mount Everest lies in the Himalayas between Nepal and Tibet. Some 70 million years ago, it lay beneath the sea, but plates in the Earth's crust have buckled to form a mountain range that is still growing, with Everest's latest "official" height put at 29,035 ft (8,850 m). It was not until 1953 that Edmund Hillary and his guide Tenzing Norgay conquered the summit, using oxygen to breathe in the thin atmosphere.

THE NORTHERN LIGHTS
Most people have seen rainbows and brilliant sunsets, but few have witnessed the amazing lights, or *aurora*, that occur near the North and the South poles. Bright colors, streaks, and flashes in the sky are caused by radiation as streams of particles from the Sun are attracted to the magnetic poles. As a result of recent air pollution, the northern lights, or *aurora borealis*, are now visible only in the most northerly parts of the Earth.

NIAGARA FALLS
The name of these spectacular falls on the border between Canada and the US may come from a Native American word meaning "thundering water." Here the Niagara River discharges enough water per minute to fill 150 Olympic swimming pools. Goat Island splits the flow of water between the Canadian or Horseshoe Fall and the smaller American Fall. The falls attract tourists and thrill-seekers: they were first crossed by tightrope walker Charles Blondin in 1859, and several people have plunged over them in special containers and survived.

THE CARLSBAD CAVERNS
The Guadalupe Mountains of New Mexico are home to the extraordinary Carlsbad Caverns. Acidic water has carved a massive network of passages and chambers through the limestone rocks to create many varied "rooms." Carlsbad is most famous for its "Big Room," one of the world's largest cave chambers at 2,000 ft (610 m) long and 1,100 ft (335 m) wide. Over the centuries, mineral-bearing water has gradually formed a variety of structures, such as stalagmites and stalactites, which grow as water drips and evaporates, leaving behind strange-looking mineral deposits.

THE GREAT BARRIER REEF

Australia's Great Barrier Reef is the world's largest coral reef and the largest ever biological structure. It extends for more than 1,250 miles (2,000 km) parallel to Queensland's northeastern coast. There are 2,900 individual reefs, 300 islets, and 210 islands within the reef, made up of 400 different types of coral. The reef has been built up over millions of years from the skeletons of marine creatures called coral polyps. Coral can grow only in clear, shallow salt water above 72° F (22° C) that is exposed to sunlight and enriched with oxygen.

This aerial view shows only a small part of the Great Barrier Reef.

THE GRAND CANYON

The five million people who visit the Grand Canyon each year are awestruck by its sheer size and beauty. Situated in northwest Arizona, the canyon is 277 miles (446 km) long and an average of 10 miles (16 km) wide. At the bottom is a stretch of the mighty Colorado River, which has carved its way through the landscape. Adding to the river's work, rainfall and streams have channelled through the rocks at different rates, depending on their hardness, to produce varied shapes and expose layers of many striking colors. One of the world's most spectacular natural wonders, its rocks reveal geological changes over millions of years. The granite rocks at the bottom of the canyon are as much as two billion years old.

The smooth walls of Uluru soar to a height of 1,142 ft (348 m). At sunset it glows a beautiful orange-red color, resembling a gigantic burning coal.

Uluru was once called Ayers Rock after the South Australian prime minister, Sir Henry Ayers. It is now known by its Aboriginal name.

ULURU

Towering over the road beneath it, Uluru is the world's largest outcrop of rock and stands in Australia's Northern Territory. Formerly known as Ayers Rock, it's made of sandstone grooved by rainwater gullies and pierced by caves. It is 2.2 miles (3.6 km) long and 1.5 miles (2 km) wide. During the day its color changes as sunlight reflects on different minerals, and it is most spectacular at sunset. Uluru is a sacred site to local people whose carvings and paintings adorn the walls of its caves.

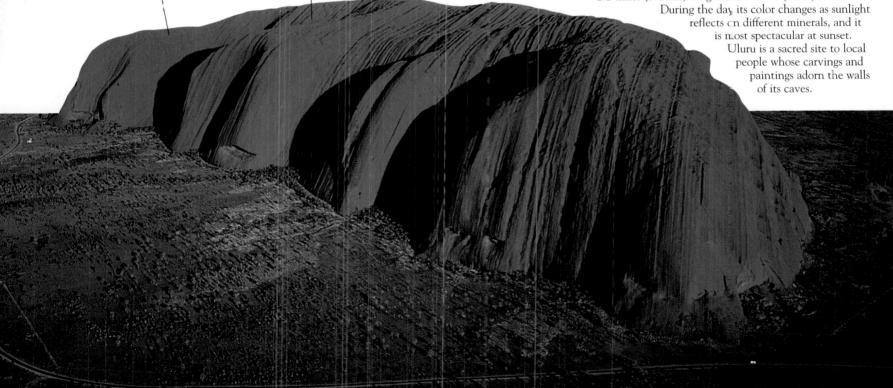

THE WONDER OF SEVEN

SEVEN HAS LONG BEEN CONSIDERED a magical number; the Babylonians identified seven planets, their temples had seven levels, and there were seven days in their week. Seven is a holy number in many religions – the Jewish candlestick or *menorah* has seven branches, and the number seven appears more than 500 times in the Bible. Perhaps because it is regarded as a lucky number, seven appears in more phrases and sayings than any other number. Seven forms part of the name of many products, such as the Boeing 747 Jumbo Jet, and the seventh son of a seventh son is said by many people to have special powers. It is most people's favourite number, and if asked to choose a number between one and 10, they are most likely to choose seven. A list of seven things is also the longest that most people can easily remember – so now you are at the end of the book, can you remember the names of all Seven Wonders of the World?

THE SEVEN DEADLY SINS

Also known as the Cardinal Sins, the Seven Deadly Sins are gluttony (greediness), sloth (laziness), lust, pride, wrath (rage), envy, and avarice (greed). They are not mentioned in the Bible, but were the sins that the Christian writer Saint Thomas Aquinas (1225–74) described as the most serious of all, for which offenders would be punished most severely.

The Seven Deadly Sins are shown here in a painting by the 15th-century artist Hieronymus Bosch.

GLUTTONY

SLOTH

AVARICE

LUST

ENVY

PRIDE

WRATH

THE SEVEN DWARFS
The well-known story of *Snow White and the Seven Dwarfs* was included by the 19th-century German writers the Brothers Grimm (Jakob and Wilhelm) among their collection of fairy tales. However, it was not until the 1937 Walt Disney film that they were called Bashful, Doc, Dopey, Grumpy, Happy, Sleepy, and Sneezy – with personalities that exactly matched their names.

MORE SEVENS

• Seven ages of man (from Shakespeare's play *As You Like It*): the infant, the whining schoolboy, the lover, the soldier, the judge, the foolish old man, and finally the second childishness and mere oblivion (death)
• Seven days of creation (according to the Bible): 1st day – light; 2nd day – heaven; 3rd day – Earth, seas, and plant life; 4th day – Sun, Moon, and stars; 5th day – sealife and birds; 6th day – land animals and humans; 7th day – God rested
• Seven days of the week: Sunday (Sun), Monday (Moon), Tuesday (Tyr, Norse god of war), Wednesday (Woden, Anglo-Saxon god), Thursday (Thor, god of Thunder), Friday (Freya, goddess of love), Saturday (Saturn, Roman god)
• Seven heavens (Islam): silver, gold, pearl, white gold, silver, ruby and garnet, and divine light
• Seven virtues (Christianity): faith, hope, charity, justice, temperance, prudence, and fortitude
• Seven continents – Africa, Antarctica, Asia, Australia, Europe, North America, and South America
• Seven heptathlon events – 100 m hurdles, high jump, shot-putting, 200 m, long jump, javelin throwing, and 800 m

SEVEN COLOURS IN A RAINBOW
Light is part of a range of radiation called the electromagnetic spectrum, which includes invisible radio waves and X-rays. White light is made up of a range of seven colours – red, orange, yellow, green, blue, indigo, and violet – but these separate colours can only be seen under special conditions. When sunlight falls on rain, the colours are split up and reflected inside the droplets to form a rainbow. Some experts say that there are only six visible colours, but the scientist Isaac Newton added indigo to get the magic seven.

INDEX

ACKNOWLEDGMENTS

Dorling Kindersley would like to thank:
Jacqueline Gooden and Robin Hunter for design assistance; Caroline Greene, Elinor Greenwood, Susan Leonard, Lee Simmons, Selina Wood, and Penny York for editorial assistance; Lynn Bresler for the index; Angela Anderson and Maureen Sheerin for additional picture research.

Picture credits
The publisher would like to thank the following for their kind permission to reproduce their photographs:

c=centre; b=bottom; l=left; r=right; t=top

Architectural Association: 49c; **The Art Archive:** 42tr, 62c; **AKG London:** 5tl; **Algemeen Nederlands Persbureau:** 54bl; **Allsport:** David Cannon 58bl; **Axiom:** Jenny Acheson 51cl; **British Museum, London:** 9crb, 15tl, 20–21; **Bruce Coleman Ltd:** Charlie Ott 60bc; Staffan Widstrand 7tr; **Colorific!:** David Mcintyre/Black Star 35br; Michael Yamashita 10cl; **James Davis Travel Photography:** 46–47, 47tc; **Mary Evans Picture Library:** 62tr; **Eye Ubiquitous:** 34tr; **Werner Forman Archive:** 27tl; **Michael Haag:** 36tr; **Robert Harding Picture Library:** 42bl; Simon Harris 11cl, 34–35; G. Hellier 23b, 41bl, 49cl; Michael Jenner 50tr; Victor Kennett 47tr; Michael Short 45t; Adina Tovy 52br; **Hulton Getty:** 5tr; **Image Bank:** Marcel Isy-Schwart 45cb; **Images Colour Library:** 62bl; David Barnes 55tr; Brian Lovell 57cb; **Jurgen Liepe:** 6bl; **National Geographic Society:** Louis Mazzatenta 49tr; **National Motor Museum, Beaulieu:** 58 cl; **Panos Pictures:** Marcus Rose 52tr; **Pictor International:** 16bl, 51b, 52tl; **Pictures Colour Library:** 20tl, 22cra, 29c, 49tl, 49br, 50bl, 51cr, 52–53, 53tr, 53bl, 56cr; **Planet Earth Pictures:** Gary Bell 61tr; **Powerstock Photolibrary/ Zefa:** A Gin 61c; © **QA Photos Ltd:** 54tl; **Rex Features:** 16cr, 22tl, 28cr, 57b, 57t; Simon Roberts 54cr; J. Sutton-Hibbert 58cr; **Scala:** 16br; **Science Museum, London:** 58tl; **Science Photo Library:** John Howard 59cra; **South American Pictures:** Kimball Morrison 57ca; Tony Morrison 52bl; **Spectrum Colour Library:** 14tl, 17bl, 40tl; G. Richardson 17br; **Frank Spooner Pictures:** Nicolas Le Corre 57tl; J Pozarik/Liaison 28–29; **Tony Stone Images:** 56b, 58ca; Robert Cameron 55bl; Fred George 40–41; David Hanson 11r; Jason Hawkes 29t; Simeone Huber 5cr; George Lepp 60cr; Mike McQueen 51t; Richard Passmore 17tr; Ed Simpson 48–49; Hugh Sitton 10c; Sarah Stone 54cl; Oliver Strewe 5b; David Sutherland 46cl; Charles Thatcher 35c; Tom Till 35t; Nabeel Turner 46bl; Larry Ulrich 61tl; **Sygma:** Joseph McNally 28bl; **Telegraph Colour Library:** 50cr; Adastra 59b; Benelux Press 59tl; Chris Bonnington 60tr; Jean-Luc Manuad/ Icone 58bc; Keren Su 48tl; Michael Freeman 46tr; Tim Graham 22cb; Travel Pix 61b; Walter Bibikow 40tr; **Topham Picturepoint:** 5tr; **Travel Ink:** Roinald Badkin 34c; Abbie Enock 60bl; Allan Hartley 23tr; **Trip:** M. Barlow 10–11.